Science and the
Renewal of Belief

Science and the Renewal of Belief

Russell Stannard

SCM PRESS LTD

334 01455 7
First published 1982
by SCM Press Ltd
58 Bloomsbury Street, London WC1

Typeset by Gloucester Typesetting Services
and printed in Great Britain by
Richard Clay Ltd (The Chaucer Press),
Bungay, Suffolk

two rivers loaded beyond belief
by gifts of a green thaw
running easily to meet
in the same sea's open arms –
O Sea!

Libby Houston

Contents

1 Introduction

The reaction on hearing that I am both a scientist and a Christian is usually one of surprise. Believers and non-believers alike find it hard to think of science and religion as being compatible with each other. It is not difficult to see why: Darwin's theory of evolution by natural selection seems to undermine the Adam and Eve story; the geological and astronomical evidence on how the universe evolved over thousands of millions of years contradicts the six-days creation story in Genesis; thunder and lightning, once regarded as manifestations of God's wrath, are now known to be nothing more than electricity; biochemists claim to be able to show that each of us is nothing but a pile of chemicals, assembled by chance rather than by design and needing no extra ingredient that can be labelled spirit or soul; miracles are an affront to the scientific laws; the very nature of scientific investigation, based as it is on sceptical reasoning and the demand for proof, contrasts with the approach one associates with religion – an approach dependent to a large extent on taking things on trust. There was the persecution of Galileo over his teachings concerning the earth going round the sun – an example, so it is held, of the way the church fights a rear-guard action against scientific advance.

These are just a selection of the problems put to me whenever I am called upon to talk about the relationship between science and religion. The people who raise these issues are those who, whilst wanting a spiritual dimension to their lives, feel that it must be one that can honestly face up to the realities of present-day scientific knowledge; they are not interested in a faith that appears to have been proved false.

My aim in this book is to demonstrate that such a belief is possible.

What I hope to show is that the alleged controversies of the past were not what they are now widely thought to have been; the very latest revelations of science, instead of posing fresh difficulties, have led to new harmony; and the methods of investigation used in science and religion, far from being opposed to each other in their outlook, are in many ways similar. Indeed, before we have finished you might well think it easier for me, as a scientist, to believe in God than it is for you!

In considering how to tackle the subject, I wondered for a time whether to try and adopt a detached point of view, setting out the arguments without allowing my own views to intrude. I decided, however, this was not practicable; such an approach would be unlikely to ring true and would, in any case, make for dull reading. So throughout I shall speak quite openly of the way I feel about each issue. But that is not to say that the book sets out to present religious belief in the best possible light. If that had been the case, I would have made a judicious selection of the topics to be included. This I have not done. Here are to be found all the major questions that have ever been put to me on the subject, including those I find awkward and for which my replies are inadequate.

I also had difficulty in deciding what to do about the purely scientific parts of the discussion. I am anxious for the book to be as widely accessible as possible – particularly to those who have no previous knowledge of science, let alone an acquaintance with some of the advanced topics to which I shall need later to refer. So the plan I have adopted is that each time I come to some new scientific idea, I shall pause and give a brief explanation of it before going on to discuss its significance. Sometimes these explanations will be no more than plain statements of the scientific findings without any attempt on my part to justify them, but occasionally I shall go a little deeper and sketch out some of the thinking behind them in order to make the conclusions more plausible; this will be so of those topics where the scientific findings are especially difficult to reconcile with commonsense ideas. I trust you will not find these parts of our discussion daunting. I have done my best to keep them short and clear. If at any time, however, you do find the going hard – my apologies. You should aim to get the general gist of what I am saying without worrying overmuch about the details. If all else fails, give it a miss for the time being and move on to the next chapter.

Much of what I have to say about the compatibility between science and religious belief applies equally to any set of religious beliefs – it is not confined to Christianity alone. Apart from the discussion of a few specifically Christian topics, such as the resurrection of Jesus and the meaning of the Trinity, readers of other faiths should for the most part be able to draw upon parallel experiences of their own.

As for what I hope you will get from our discussion, that will rather depend upon you. If you already believe in God, then you will find here an opportunity to reassess your beliefs in the light of modern thought. This is unlikely to be easy; exposing long-cherished convictions to sceptical reappraisal can be a painful process. You might not like the way I go about it; for example my attitude towards the Bible might strike you as lacking in reverence, my interpretation of various miracles harsh, my rejection of so-called proofs of God's existence distressing. But some hurt is unavoidable if certain aspects of belief are found to lack integrity and so ought to be discarded. And discarded they must be if you are to reconstruct for yourself a strong faith built only on what is true, essential and in keeping with our modern understanding of the world.

If, on the other hand, you do not believe in God, you must not expect me to argue you into doing so. No one comes to know God by passively sitting back reading books or listening to arguments, no matter how cleverly and persuasively they might have been devised. Coming to know God involves active participation (the subject of a later chapter). The objective of this book, so far as you are concerned, is not to bring about your conversion, desirable though that might be, but the more modest one of removing some of the obstacles that might be in your path at present. When this is done, you will find that, whatever additional reasons you think you have for not taking the necessary step towards making contact with God, an incompatibility between science and religion cannot legitimately be counted as one of them.

One final point: I have avoided cluttering up the text with references and footnotes. This is a book for enjoyment as well as for study; it is not a textbook and I did not want it to look like one. There is, however, a list at the back for anyone who wishes to look up biblical quotations and other references.

2 In the Beginning

Where shall we begin? I suggest we make a start with that topic that must loom large in any discussion of science and religion: Darwin's theory of evolution. Deciding whether we descended from Adam and Eve, or from more primitive ancestors, immediately faces us with the need to look into the credibility of the Bible. Some Christians shy away from doing this, perhaps because they consider it disrespectful – perhaps because they are fearful of what such an examination might reveal. But it is an issue that in all honesty must be faced at some time and it might just as well be sooner as later.

The biblical account of our origin is well known and there is no need to spend time recounting its details. The story of how Adam came into existence fully formed on the sixth day of creation and how Eve made her appearance somewhat later through God fashioning a rib taken from Adam's side, is familiar to us all.

Darwin's alternative proposal is likewise common knowledge, at least as far as its main claims are concerned. The basic ideas as to how we descended from the same ancestors as the apes can be summarized as follows.

In every species there are differences between its individual members. Some are faster in running than others, or have sharper claws, a thicker protective skin, better eyesight, or greater intelligence; others are less fortunate. Those lucky enough to possess a characteristic that improves their chances of avoiding predators or finding scarce food are the ones likely to survive to an age where they can mate and have offspring. There is therefore a weeding-out process between birth and mating. Those that become parents will not be truly representative of those that were born. On average they will be better suited for survival.

And those same superior qualities that contributed to their own survival will tend to be inherited by the next generation.

Suppose, for example, the important quality determining survival is speed of movement. The members of a particular generation will have a distribution of speeds about some mean value. The faster members are more likely to survive to have offspring than the slower ones who tend to fall victim to predators. The average speed of those who succeed in becoming parents will therefore be somewhat higher than the average for their generation as a whole. These parents will then proceed to produce a new generation with an average speed similar to their own, which, as we have seen, is somewhat higher than the average speed of the generation to which the parents belonged. Thus the average speed has increased. Moreover, the process is all set to be repeated when this second generation gives rise to the third and so on.

Here, then, we have a mechanism for steadily improving the characteristics conducive to survival. Note that the theory of evolution does not require any Over-seeing Intelligence directing operations. All changes occur randomly; it is the unthinking process of natural selection that acts as the automatic sieve ensuring that the beneficial characteristics have the greater chance of being preserved and further developed in succeeding generations.

The process would appear to work at any level from the most primitive forms of life to the most sophisticated. It is tempting, therefore, to presume that all the higher forms of life we see about us today – ourselves included – have evolved from humble origins. This being so, the theory of evolution by natural selection offers an alternative to the Adam and Eve story.

The experimental evidence for evolution is strong. For example, the fossil records allow us, through a study of ancient bones and the imprints left by animals in rocks, to trace the emergence and extinction of species. They disclose how one kind of animal developed into another. Gaps in the record tracing back man's ancestors admittedly do occur. But these can hardly be held to discredit the theory. Progressively the gaps are being filled, several notable finds having been made in the last ten years or so.

Secondly, the process of evolution can be seen to be in operation in our own time. Moths living in dirty industrial areas, for instance, are darker in colour than they were in former times. This appears to be due to the way that the moths which happen by chance to be somewhat darker than average are better camouflaged on the increasingly grimy surfaces on which they habitually rest. The difficulty in seeing these moths gives them an improved chance of escaping the attention of predator birds. The surviving moths then pass on their darker colouring to their offspring and, with each succeeding generation, the effect becomes more marked. Another well-known example of evolution in action today is the way certain strains of flies and mosquitoes have acquired immunity from DDT. Indeed, there have been quite a number of recent instances of pests developing a resistance to the chemicals intended for their control.

Not only is the experimental evidence for evolution much stronger now than it was at the time Darwin set out his ideas, there have also been important advances on the theoretical side. Work in the field of molecular biology, as we shall discuss in greater detail later, has revealed the actual physical mechanism by which the characteristics of heredity are passed on and how, in the process, the characteristics acquire the random variations upon which natural selection works.

Is there no evidence *against* the theory? Laying aside objections based solely on the assertion that a literal interpretation of Genesis must be adhered to at all costs, there would appear to be only one objection meriting serious attention. This is concerned with the question of degree. Whilst accepting that a measure of evolution has clearly taken place in the past and continues to occur in the present, one can argue that it does not follow that something as complex as the eye, the ear, or the brain could have evolved in this manner. Darwin himself expressed reservations on this score. In his book *On the Origin of Species* he wrote:

> To suppose that the eye with all its inimitable contrivances for adjusting the focus to different distances, for admitting different amounts of light, and for the correction of spherical and chromatic abberation, could have been formed by natural selection, seems, I freely confess, absurd in the highest degree . . .

And yet he was to go on to claim, a little later in the same book, that provided one could show that between the simplest example of an eye and its final perfect form there could exist gradations, each of which would have been useful to the animal, the eye could indeed have so developed.

The evolution of intricate structures in terms of innumerable slight modifications would obviously take a long time: millions and millions of years. Has there, in fact, been sufficient time for all this to happen?

It is here we find the Bible confronted by a second challenge: not only does the Bible speak of us as being descended from Adam and Eve, it would appear to allow us to work out when these ancient ancestors lived. Such a calculation has been made. It is to be found printed on the back cover of an eighteenth century family Bible I once possessed and is headed: 'A Chronological Index of the Years and Times from Adam unto Christ, Proved by Scriptures'. The compiler of the index industriously adds the age of Adam when he begat Seth, to that of Seth when he begat Enosh, to that of Enosh when he begat Kenan, and so on, right through all the relevant Old Testament figures. He ends triumphantly with the conclusion: 'Whereupon we reckon that from Adam unto Christ are three thousand, nine hundred and seventy four years, six months and ten days.' Even with the extra ten days, that is hardly enough for Darwin's purposes!

What does the geologist have to say? Modern research into the dating of rocks using radio-active techniques sets the age of the earth at over 4,000 *million* years. Not only does this make a nonsense of biblical chronology, it provides the process of evolution essentially an unlimited span of time and so lends further credence to Darwin's theory.

As though this were not enough, to the findings of biology and geology there have been added, over the past fifty years, those of astronomy. According to the evidence of the telescope, the universe began with a violent explosion: the so-called Big Bang. The explosion flung out the matter of the universe in the form of a searingly hot gas. On expanding, it cooled and gathered together to form galaxies. These are great swirling collections of stars. Around some of the stars planets formed. One such star was the sun. The galaxies are still hurtling away from each other in the aftermath of the original explosion and in recent years the telescopes have even revealed the remnants of the bright blinding flash of light that accompanied the universe's violent birth.

8

Observation of the speeds of the galaxies and of their present positions allows one to estimate how long ago the Big Bang occurred. The age of the universe comes out to be about 15,000 million years. This is somewhat greater than the age of the earth which, of course, is how it should be – some time would have elapsed between the moment of creation and the beginning of the condensation process which led to the formation of the planet.

Thus the independent researches of the biologist, geologist and astronomer unite to provide a mutually consistent account of past history – and it is not remotely like that offered by Genesis.

How do I as a scientist react to these various discoveries? I have no option; I must abide by the scientific evidence. That is not to say I necessarily believe my fellow scientists to have a wholly truthful picture; some conjecturing is still involved. The original ideas of Darwin have been subsequently modified in their details and indeed are currently being challenged by a number of biologists. None of this criticism, however, is aimed at restoring biblical creationism – even among the critics, evolution is still accepted as an established fact. Instead, the controversy is confined to arguments about how exactly evolution has taken place. For instance, did the significant changes occur only gradually, or did they take place in a series of steps interspersed with periods of comparatively little change? Likewise, the time-scale of the universe has been revised at least once since the first estimate was made from observations on the movements of the galaxies. But once again the amendments and improvements have been relatively minor, the main features of the picture undergoing no radical change. To my mind, we are in possession of an essentially accurate account of the history of the world and of the origins of man.

So what does acceptance of the scientific view imply for Genesis? Can one any longer, with integrity, accord it the kind of respect Christians have traditionally shown it? Bishop Wilberforce, in a famous pronouncement in 1860, made it clear how he himself felt:

The principle of natural selection is absolutely incompatible with the word of God. If its thesis is true, Genesis is a lie. The whole framework of the book of life falls to pieces, and the revelation of God to man as we Christians know it is a delusion and a snare.

Darwin did not agree. In his book *On the Origin of Species* to which I referred earlier, he wrote: 'I see no good reasons why the views given in this volume should shock the religious feelings of anyone.' As I now hope to show, Darwin was right in this assessment.

3 On How to Interpret the Bible

As a preliminary to looking at the Bible, let me ask you to guess who might have said the following:

> In the beginning were created only germs or causes of the forms of life which were afterwards to be developed in gradual course.

Surprisingly, the answer is not the obvious one; it was not Darwin, nor indeed any modern evolutionist. The words were spoken by St Augustine 1,400 years earlier. According to Augustine, everything in the world was created in a single moment. But all living things, whether plant, animal, or man, were only pre-formed, made 'invisibly, potentially, causally, as future things which have not been made are made.' The world was created like a mother-to-be, pregnant with the causes of beings yet to come. The Genesis reference to six days of creation, followed by a day of rest, was symbolic – an accommodation to the weakness of our imagination. Instead of being an account of what had actually happened in the past, it was rather to be seen as foretelling seven ages of the world that were yet to come.

No one was more influential in the early church than Augustine; he shaped theology down to the Middle Ages. He still commands our respect today; in the 1950s, for example, over seventy new books appeared analysing various aspects of his thinking. He was not alone in his interpretation of Genesis. Though it is true that the doctrine of God as creator, together with other beliefs (such as those concerning the nature of the man-woman relationship and the status of man in the animal kingdom), were all derived from Genesis, that is not to say the early church held to a literal interpretation of those writings. The lack of literal intention was in fact repeatedly asserted by many of the early church fathers – not only by Augustine.

None of this, of course, should be misconstrued to mean that the early church leaders knew about evolution by natural selection before Darwin – they clearly did not. But what is certain is that the evidence for evolution, had it come to light around AD 400, would have caused no shock. On the contrary, it would have been regarded as wholly in keeping with the views of the church.

So it is that we are led to ask how it came about that the actual reception given to Darwin's theory was so different. Why did certain Christians, like Wilberforce, feel compelled to defend a literal interpretation of Genesis – one that was not shared by the early church? Indeed, why do so many Christians adopt the same stand today?

Unqualified acceptance of the literal approach to the Bible did not, in fact, become established until a comparatively late date: the sixteenth century – the time of the Reformation.

The Reformation came about not, as many today would believe, simply because Henry the Eighth wanted a divorce. Though the divorce was admittedly the immediate trigger for the break with Rome, at least as far as the English were concerned, there were earlier and much more deep-seated causes. Among these was a growing feeling that too much authority had become invested in the Pope and that the balance needed to be redressed. The Protestants, led by Martin Luther from about 1517, held there to be but one over-riding authority – the Bible; they stood by the teachings of the Bible and by nothing else. Not to be outdone, those remaining loyal to Rome denied that recognition of Papal authority in any way diminished their esteem for scripture. The Council of Trent was set up in the 1540s primarily with the object of making plain the Roman Catholic position on those aspects of belief challenged by the Protestants. A decree was issued stating that God was the 'author' of both the Old and New Testaments. The Council went on to declare that the New Testament writings had been produced 'at the dictation of the Holy Spirit'. Thus, over the years, perhaps without anyone consciously realizing what was happening, opposing groups of Christians manoeuvred each other into defending positions whereby the genuineness of one's belief became dependent upon how firmly one stood by the Bible; or to put it more crudely, how much of the Bible could be swallowed without questions being asked. In this way, the literal interpretation of books such as Genesis came to be uncritically accepted.

It could only be a matter of time before the folly was exposed – the kind of folly to be found in the pronouncements of people like Bishop Wilberforce. Not that Wilberforce spoke for the church as a whole. Though many were indeed disturbed by Darwin's proposals, it is only fair to point out that there were others who readily embraced the theory. The theologian, Stewart Headlam, for example, spoke for many when in 1879, twenty years after the appearance of *On the Origin of Species*, he said:

> Thank God that the scientific men have . . . shattered the idol of the infallible book . . . It gives us far grander notions of God to think of him making the world by his Spirit through the ages than to think of him making it in a few days.

Frederick Temple, later to be Archbishop of Canterbury, was another of the more enlightened thinkers. In 1884, he gave a series of lectures in Oxford in which he assumed the truth of the theory of evolution to be self-evident. And, of course, we must not overlook the fact that when Darwin died in 1882, he was accorded the honour of burial in Westminster Abbey. In short, despite the initial doubts of some churchmen – doubts, I hasten to add, shared by a number of scientists of the time who were unconvinced on purely scientific grounds that Darwin had proved his case – most Christians, in a relatively short time, came to accept the validity of the theory of evolution.

But where does that leave the Bible? If Genesis is not meant to be literally true, in what sense, if any, is it to be regarded as truthful and of value?

Before attempting an assessment of the Bible, one ought to recognize from the outset that it is a book that can be read and appreciated at various levels of understanding. I would not like to give the impression from what follows that I am claiming one has to be a biblical scholar in order to grasp its basic message; that is not the case – the youngest child can read at least certain passages and stories with understanding. But to tackle the book in a *critical* frame of mind – which is what we shall attempt to do – is a quite different matter. The Bible is full of pit-falls for the unwary amateur critic. For someone untrained in biblical criticism, it is as unwise to make assertions about its alleged errors and absurdities as it would be for someone who knows no physics to hold forth on where Einstein 'went wrong' in his theory of relativity.

In what follows, I shall give you just a hint of some of the difficulties involved. We shall not delve too deeply – for the simple reason that I am not myself a biblical scholar and so should heed my own warning! All I can do is pass on to you something of what I have learned in my own reading of the subject. We shall venture just far enough to allow us to appreciate why the recent scientific advances I have described do not in any way represent a challenge to the true message of the Bible.

Firstly, we note that the Bible is not, strictly speaking, a book – it is a library of books. Who the authors of the various volumes were we often do not know. Certain of the books are clearly drawn from more than one source and have several authors. This in itself can strike the modern reader as odd. Questions of authorship are for us all-important; for the early Hebrew writers it was not so. In those days, writers were allowed freely to quote passages from the works of others without acknowledgment. What today would be regarded as an infringement of copyright and would lead to a court action, in those days would have been regarded as a compliment – what greater tribute could one author pay another, it would be argued, than for him to want to pass off the other's work as his own! It all depends on custom and how one has been brought up to regard such matters.

Next, we must appreciate that not only were the books of the Bible written by different authors, but also they are examples of almost every kind of literature: history, poems, legends, songs, proverbs, statements of the law, orations, biographies, genealogical records and collections of letters. No one today would go into a public library, choose books at random from all the sections, and sit down to read each volume in exactly the same frame of mind as every other one in the selection. In a scientific textbook, for example, one looks for an unambiguous, matter-of-fact account of phenomena that have actually been observed to occur. The same expectation of a book of poetry would be out of place: 'the girl's eyes flash with fire' is a ridiculous assertion if viewed literally, but perfectly acceptable in the context of a poem. Not only acceptable, but a more effective means of conveying the essential nature of the girl's passion than, say, a scientific measurement of the enlargement of her pupils. But for this type of communication to be established, there must be a willingness on the part of the reader to accommodate his or her approach to the book so that it conforms to the intentions of the author. What is true of poetry applies equally to the novel. Here, again, we find that profound insights into the human condition can be provided through a medium which is, in a sense, 'untruthful' – through the use of characters who never existed and events that never took place. Once again, there need be no difficulty in arriving at what is true and what is not; we merely have to be alerted to the conventions adopted by novelists. So we find that each book in our library selection is potentially capable of conveying some truth about ourselves and about the world we inhabit. But this potential can only be realized if we, the readers, are on the same wavelength as each writer.

A further problem encountered in making the right approach to the Bible is that some of its books were written according to ancient traditions that have no counterpart today. Having, for instance, established that a particular book is largely historical in character, it is not necessarily appropriate that one should approach it as one would a modern history book. The modern historian attempts to give an accurate, authoritative account of certain events that occurred in the past. His intention is to be objective. Admittedly this might not be easy; his own views are liable to colour both his record of what happened and also his interpretation of why it happened. His account of the Russian revolution, for example, might disagree in important respects from that of some other historian of a different political persuasion. He has to be selective in his facts, it being impossible to give an exhaustive account of everything that has occurred, and the very act of choosing what to include involves a value judgment that can lead to bias. But regardless of how successful he might be, his intention is clear: he tries to produce a faithful record of events that actually occurred.

Not so the early Jewish historian. The prime purpose of historical writing for him was to show God working out his purpose in the history of man. History was theology and the interpretation of events was to be made in that context. His writing was intended to uplift and inspire his readers. To this end, he felt justified in adapting his account to conform more closely to what he considered *ought* to have happened! One of his aims was to hold up before the youth of his day fine examples of ancestors upon whom they could model themselves. It became common practice for notable deeds performed by descendants of the founder of the tribe to be transposed in time and accorded to the venerated founder himself. In this way great victories were won – posthumously. The practice became so common that it is now impossible to unscramble what the ancestor himself actually did. Doubt has even been cast on whether certain prominent Old Testament characters, such as Moses and Israel, existed at all; they might merely be symbolic figures embodying the achievements of the nation as a whole. Then there was the question of a person's age. Unlike today, when children pay scant respect to their parents and grandparents and a man is spoken of as 'finished at forty', in former times age was synonymous with wisdom. The greater a person's age, the more experience he must have had of life and so, the argument ran, the more he should be revered as a sage. In the cause of honouring one's ancestors, therefore, what could be more appropriate than to add a few years to their recorded age – and then, one suspects, a few more for good measure!

The exercise of such freedom in the writing of historical narrative is alien to us today. Poetic licence we are happy to accept; historical licence seems somehow wrong and dishonest. But is there really any harm in it – provided, of course, that the reader is accustomed to the style and does not accord the writings a literal significance they were never intended to carry? Could it not be argued that our own historical accounts are, by comparison, dull, prosaic and lacking in imaginative flair and purpose? To the early Jewish writers they would certainly have appeared so.

This somewhat cavalier approach to straight historical facts, whilst making for exhilarating reading, can cause no end of problems for those trying to come to terms with the Bible. It would not be so bad if all the historical books were written in this vein; once one had been made aware of what was going on, one could adjust one's attitude to them and all would be well. But this is not the case. Although the early books were written in this unfamiliar style, the later ones were not, or at least not to the same extent. We must not overlook the fact that

Christianity is fundamentally an historical religion; whether certain events in the life of Jesus, such as the resurrection, actually occurred or not are key questions. Sorting out those biblical writings that are intended to be factually correct from those that are of a more inspirational character is no easy matter, but is something that has to be attempted.

Before ending these cautionary words on the difficulties of interpreting the Bible, I need to say a little about the use of myth, for it is with myth that we are concerned in the early chapters of Genesis. Today the term 'myth' conjures up a totally misleading impression. If, in normal conversation, we call something a myth, we mean that it is untrue. But this is not the way the word is used when applied to the Bible. Whilst there is no denying that the biblical myths describe events that did not occur in any historical sense, that is not the point; they never professed to be accounts of that nature. The symbolic language in which they are couched is but a vehicle – a means of transmitting what really matters: their deep underlying truths. These truths were held to be timeless; they applied to all generations and for this reason were highly valued.

Why use myths rather than some more straightforward way of passing on the fruits of a nation's experience to succeeding generations? We must recall that myths came into being at a time when communication was almost exclusively by word of mouth, most people being unable to read or write. Such a state of affairs today would make the reliable transmission of information from one generation to the next virtually impossible. Anyone who has played the party-game of whispering a message into one person's ear, for that person then to pass it on to the next, will be aware of how garbled the message can become by the time it has been round the room (even without the help of those along the line who distort it deliberately!). But it would be wrong to ascribe to ancient people a similar inability to remember verbal messages accurately. The oral tradition of the past was developed into a highly effective means of communication. Its reliability was far beyond anything we ourselves would credit possible. Partly its efficiency derived from a disciplined approach to remembering verbal messages, in contrast to today's move away from learning by rote, and partly it was due to the nature of the message itself – the myth. The myth was designed to be memorable. It described events that were out-of-the-ordinary. It was kept short and was conceived in language vivid in its imagery. The Jews were not alone in using myths; many ancient civilizations employed them. Indeed, the myths of creation and of Noah's flood are believed to have been taken into Genesis from the traditions of other nations.

This being the nature of myths, it makes no more sense to subject them to scientific and historical analysis than it would to treat a poem or novel in that way. But most attacks on Genesis are founded on just such a misconception. Scientific investigations highlighting the lack of literal truth in the myths, reveal nothing new. They expose no falsehood, but merely remind us of the need to return to the original and largely forgotten ways of interpreting these writings.

So, with these thoughts in mind, let us turn our attention to the early chapters of Genesis with a view to trying to uncover their true message.

4 The Message of the Myths

To establish the context of the Adam and Eve story, we need first to look briefly at the accounts of creation. Note I say 'accounts' in the plural – it is not universally recognized that Genesis contains two of them. (If you are unsure of this, take a look; you will find the second account commencing at chapter 2, verse 4.) The editor of Genesis could not but have realized that he was placing two somewhat inconsistent accounts one after the other; the fact that he saw fit to do so is reason enough for concluding that they were not meant to be taken literally.

The first important declaration to be made by the creation myths is that there is a God; behind the created world there lies a Divine Presence. That there should be only one God, rather than a multitude of them, is in itself noteworthy; most ancient civilizations held there to be many gods, some associated with different aspects of life and others with different tribes and locations. The Genesis assertion of a single all-powerful creator God provides, in contrast, an underlying unity to all nature. Man himself is included within this unity; he is depicted as being formed in the image of God – he is God's representative on earth. As such he enjoys the privilege of a close relationship with the creator; God takes a personal interest in his well-being. The whole of creation is seen to be good. All is perfect and harmonious.

A more confident and reassuring appraisal it would be hard to imagine. One is left wondering where the evidence to support it is to be found. Has its author not heard of earthquakes, floods, famine, disease, war and crime? Would it not be easier to come to precisely the opposite view and conclude that the world is characterized by disunity, man at odds with his environment and with his fellow-man, and God – if he exists at all – at best unconcerned for man's fate and, at worst, malevolent? That is, after all, how the Greeks saw their gods – deities that could be spiteful, immoral and capricious. And yet, in the face of what might seem to us strong evidence to the contrary, Genesis insists on its own highly individual assessment of God, man and creation, and of the relationship between them.

Simplistic optimism? No. Before jumping to a conclusion like that, we must recognize that all we have looked at so far is the prelude; the drama has yet to come. In what follows, we find that the problem of evil and suffering, far from having been ignored, is actually the prime focus. The function of the Adam and Eve myth is indeed to provide an answer to the question: 'Why, if God and all creation is essentially good, does man as God's representative so consistently fall short of his intended role?'

On the surface, the story has an almost child-like simplicity; but appearances are deceptive. The deeper one probes, the more one realizes that it is anything but naive. For instance, could any modern scientific account of the origins of life on earth give a better feel for the intimate relationship between man and the planet he inhabits than the words, 'God fashioned man of dust from the soil'? Or what more poignant image could be devised for characterizing the union of man and wife than that in which Eve is described as being built from the very material of Adam's body?

But let us go to the heart of the story. The action is straightforward: Adam and Eve are placed in Paradise; all is perfect and could remain so indefinitely provided they remain obedient to God's will. But then comes the act of disobedience, the eating of the forbidden fruit, and this leads to their being driven from the Garden of Eden. The banishment is permanent: never again are they to enter Paradise. They henceforth live under a kind of curse, permanently alienated from God, the source of all goodness. The sentence pronounced on Adam and Eve applies also to their descendants, which, of course, means you and me. So the nub of the story, as it affects us, is that, no matter how hard we strive to live up to our intended role as God's representative, we are destined to fail; we fail because in some essential way we are alienated from God and his goodness for a reason that has to do with something that lies buried in the past – an occurrence over which we have no control. Because of some basic defect built into us from the very beginning, we are unable to live wholly good lives and are therefore unable to create for ourselves a paradise on earth. This inherent bias towards falling short of perfection goes under the name 'original sin'.

I find there is nothing quite like original sin for getting people's backs up! One instinctively recoils from the very idea that a baby could be regarded as sinful. Surely a baby at birth must by its very nature be pure, innocent and free from all tendencies towards evil. When it subsequently develops into the teenage hooligan on the football terraces, it can only be due to the way it has become corrupted by bad external influences – a broken home, say, or violence shown on television. If only such influences could be eliminated, so it is argued, would not all be well? The answer of Genesis is: no.

No one denies that many changes are in themselves desirable: the improvement in working conditions; increased leisure hours; the way schools have become much pleasanter places than they used to be; the reduction in sex discrimination; the fight against racial bigotry; the freeing of women from much domestic drudgery; the rise in the standard of living and the manner in which poverty – true poverty – has been reduced, at least in the more advanced countries. But to what extent have these changes resulted in our being happier? Are we any the more content? How much closer are we to establishing a paradise on earth? To judge from the soaring crime statistics, the incidence of mental depression and the numbers driven to commit suicide, the prevalence of industrial disputes, and our ordinary day-to-day observations of the way people behave towards one another, it would seem not much closer, if at all. Even the most determined efforts to set up an enclosed, private paradise involving like-minded, idealistic people – whether it be in the form of a commune, a kibbutz, an exclusive school, a club or society, a marriage, a political state, a monastic order or new church – all such efforts seem doomed to fail and something short of perfection results. It is rather like a farmer who selects the very best fruit from his harvest and seeks to preserve them indefinitely by sealing them in a container to protect them from harm; on opening them up later, he finds they have still rotted, the source of decay having lain within rather than without.

Persuasive though it undoubtedly is to regard oneself as intrinsically good whilst blaming all troubles on bad external influences, such an approach does not get to the root of the problem of the existence of evil. Rather against my will, I have found myself coming progressively to the view that, for whatever reason, the source of the problem does indeed lie within us, just as Genesis would have it. That is not to say I advocate sitting back and doing nothing about the environment and bad influences. Of course not. Such influences exacerbate the problem. But they are not themselves the source; their effect is confined to aggravating a condition that would still persist even though they were eliminated.

Whether one likes it or not, original sin is one of the underpinning concepts of Christianity. Until recent times, it has been an article of belief that has rested solely on the assertion made by Genesis, backed up perhaps by one's own experience of life. As a Christian, one has had to accept, more or less blindly, that for reasons unknown man consistently lapses into selfishness and falls short of what one suspects might be his true potential. I say 'until recent times', because I believe that the situation has now changed. Science, far from having undermined the basic thesis of the Adam and Eve myth, has now provided the first rational understanding of it. It provides not one, but *two* contributing reasons why the myth is likely to be true. In both cases, they are concerned with events that have happened in the past over which we have no control; both give rise to a tendency towards self-centredness and a disregard for the needs and rights of others – a tendency to which can be attributed most, if not all, of the difficulties encountered in human relationships. It is to these scientific developments we now turn.

5 Adam and Eve in a New Light

The first of these scientific insights comes from an unexpected quarter: the theory of evolution by natural selection. The theory, which has already drawn attention to the need to regard the Adam and Eve story as something other than a literal account of man's origins, goes on to provide a way of appreciating its underlying message. To see how this comes about, we must take a closer look at Darwin's theory and the manner in which it has been subsequently developed through more recent research.

At the time Darwin proposed his theory, little was known either about the mechanism by which inherited characteristics were passed on from one generation to the next, or about the cause of those random variations upon which the principle of natural selection worked. It has now been shown that the determining agent in the process is a particular kind of molecule, that is to say, a particular arrangement of atoms. Its name is customarily, and I would add mercifully, abbreviated to its initial letters: DNA. The DNA molecule consists of a long chain, or sequence, of smaller molecules arranged in the form of two intertwined helices (looking rather like two interlocked bed-springs). Its important property is that the order and position in which the smaller molecules appear along the chain constitutes a code – a code which determines the physical characteristics of the organism. There exists, moreover, a means of duplicating the DNA molecules so that copies of the codes can be transcribed and used to build up the DNA molecules of offspring. The reason why parents and offspring resemble each other is that similar DNA codings are to be found in each. As for the random variations upon which natural selection works, these can be attributed to mistakes in the copying procedure and, occasionally, to alterations to the molecular structures caused by the effects of radiation.

Physical characteristics such as height, colour of eyes and hair, level of intelligence and so on, are not the only attributes to be passed on from parent to offspring; as part of the inheritance there comes an array of instincts. It is of little use for an animal to be endowed with some physical advantage if it does not know how to use it. The process of evolution passes on, therefore, a set of mental attitudes and behavioural characteristics that do not have to be learnt. Each animal is, to some extent, pre-programmed with a basic knowledge of how it should behave in order to maximize its chances of survival. Such instincts might reveal themselves as an immediate ability to swim, or through the instant recognition and fear of potential predators, or through competence at locating suitable food. How many children, I wonder, have been shocked to see their well-fed kitten tormenting and unnecessarily killing a mouse or bird it has caught? How did it learn such cruel behaviour? The answer is that it did not learn it; what is being observed is an automatic response to a deep-seated, inborn instinct – one that is thought to be encoded in the kitten's DNA molecules.

Much of the instinctive drive found in the animal kingdom centres on mating. Males will engage in contests as they rival with each other for the attention of the females. Fights tend to be won by the stronger, so it falls to the superior males to father the young. This type of selection will lead to offspring that are similarly well-endowed because they will take after their father. Though this might be considered unfair and inconsiderate of the 'rights' of the less fortunate males, natural selection has no respect for such niceties. For certain species, lions for example, the dominance of selected males can be taken to limits that are quite repugnant to our sensibilities. A lion, having won the rights over a group of lionesses, has to be prepared to fight off rivals if he is to retain them; in the event of a stronger male coming on to the scene, he forfeits them. But not content with having won the females, the newcomer, in response to a basic instinct, will now systematically bite to death any cubs fathered by the previous male. By this action, he stops the lionesses expending time and effort caring for the progeny of the other lion and frees them to devote their attention to the needs of his own. This makes sense in evolutionary terms because the only surviving cubs will now be those of the second male – the stronger of the two – and so liable to be the stronger of the cubs that have been born. In addition to inheriting their father's strength, these cubs will also have passed on to them his set of instincts, so they in turn, on reaching maturity, are set to repeat the same pattern of behaviour.

Though most instincts are concerned with the self-interest of the individual and could therefore be judged from a moral stand-point to be 'selfish', this is not invariably the rule. Sometimes instincts give rise to animal behaviour that is self-sacrificing and which, if it were to occur in a human being, would be regarded as highly moral and commendable. A mother, for instance, might sacrifice her own life by diverting the attention of a predator away from her offspring and towards herself. Such instinctive behaviour, although it works against the survival of the individual, can nevertheless be understood in evolutionary terms. The mother, having already passed on her characteristics to her offspring, is, in a sense, expendable; what matters now is that the offspring should survive. The instinct that drives the mother to sacrifice herself is therefore, somewhat paradoxically, that which ensures the perpetuation of that self-same instinct in the next generation. For similar reasons, the sterile worker bee will kill itself, through stinging a potential enemy, in order to protect the fertile queen. Contemporary evolutionists study all these kinds of seemingly 'altruistic' behaviour and their work indicates that selection can take place not only between individuals, but also at the level of families and of communities sharing the same hereditary material. Selection also takes place lower down the scale of organic complexity at the level of individual cells – the dominance gained by cancer cells over normal cells being an example.

But whilst acknowledging that evolution can take place at different levels and in the process can give rise to a wide range of instinctive responses, modern evolutionists still maintain that the dominant evolutionary activity is, in all probability, still to be found at the level where competition and selection takes place between individuals. This is just as Darwin had originally supposed. The survival and development of the species remains identified with the self-interest of the individual and of his own offspring. In this way, one comes to expect that, although to some degree there might evolve instincts that appear from a moral stand-point altruistic, most when so judged would be of a type that was self-seeking.

What, you might ask, has all this to do with man? Simply this: it is inconceivable that man, alone among the animals, has not inherited an array of instincts. Our distant ancestors were engaged in the same struggle to survive as the other animals of the time; if the other animals required a set of instincts as an integral part of their survival kit, our ancestors must surely have needed them too. Furthermore, if those instincts in other animals are seen now, in the main, to be self-seeking, the same is likely to be true of our own. I believe this conclusion to be inescapable. Moreover, I do not think one has to look far to find the evidence for it. Examples of competitiveness and aggression abound: participation in sports, aiming to come top in an examination, working to gain promotion, endeavouring to expand a commercial business, organizing a strike for higher wages, establishing a relationship with a desirable member of the opposite sex in the face of competition from a rival and, of course, the act of going to war. In all cases, the aim, directly or indirectly, is to gain some advantage at the expense of another. Further, I am not persuaded that our self-seeking instincts are any the less pronounced than those of other animals. One hears it said, for instance, that we have a natural inclination towards adopting a 'moral' attitude over the question of finding a sexual partner. Unlike certain other animals, we believe in one-man-for-one-woman and so are not drawn towards the 'excesses' to be found among polygamous species – those lions, for example. I would not be so sure about this. A characteristic feature of polygamous species is that the males tend to be somewhat bigger and physically stronger than the females, this arising from the greater element of selection among the males. Could the difference between the average size and strength of the sexes in our own species point to us not being as monogamous as we would like to think? Some scientists believe that our distant ancestors were to some extent polygamous and that this tendency might linger in us today. Though we might not bite our step-children to death, I suspect that echoes of past competitions between males over the polygamous possession of females could go a long way towards explaining the otherwise curious fact that men are more overtly aggressive than females, if one is to judge from crime statistics and from their greater participation in the more violent sports, boxing and wrestling.

In summary, therefore, I would hold that in order to understand man's behaviour one must accept that he is in part driven by instincts. Indelibly written into his DNA molecules are coded messages associated with innate behaviour – behaviour that is a relic of the ruthless, cruel struggle his ancestors fought in order to survive, a struggle that made modern man's own existence possible. And just as we see in other species the 'rights' of the individual made subservient to the self-interest of the more favoured members, so this same tendency is at work in the cruelty that man consistently shows towards his fellow-man. Thus, the behaviour patterns regarded as 'sinful' – those based on self-interest and a disregard for others – are the very same patterns programmed into us from the moment of conception.

The originator of the Adam and Eve story, of course, knew nothing of this; he had no way of telling why we behave the way we do. And yet he identified with remarkable insight the root of the problem. He knew that the real source of our sinful tendencies lay within us and not in external influences. Regardless of how the environment and social conditions might be improved, important and helpful though these could be, he knew that such remedies only scratch the surface; man lives in the grip of an irresistible influence which dooms to failure all his attempts to live selflessly as God's representative on earth. Whether one chooses to ascribe that influence to the actions of someone in the past called Adam, or to the actions of ancestral ape-like creatures, seems to me immaterial. The message is the same: the source of sin lies within each one of us.

In this way, I find no conflict between the Adam and Eve story and the theory of evolution by natural selection. At the level where they speak of the present condition of mankind, they are completely in accord. One of the things I find so satisfying about Darwin's theory and the experimental evidence for it, is the way it provides us at last with a firm understanding of the scientific and historical basis of the truth behind the myth.

This, of course, is not the way Christian fundamentalists see it. Their view, that one must hold to a literal interpretation of Genesis at all costs, is one that has come to be heard with increasing insistence in recent years. Especially is this the case in those states in the USA where attempts have been made to impose the creation account on the schools' curricula. To some extent I appreciate the feelings of such people. They have a deep reverence for the Bible and it is right and proper that this should be so. They see the danger that once one starts to question one aspect of the Bible, it is not clear where this process will stop. Even I, who am regarded as having rather liberal views in such matters, on occasion get riled by certain modern theologians who (so I think) are excessively sceptical. Too much emphasis on the 'difficulties' and 'pitfalls' of understanding the Bible can lead to lay people not reading the Bible for themselves; it can make believers reluctant to speak up for their faith; it can create the impression of a religion that does not know what it stands for. But the answer to these natural concerns is not that one should cling to a literal interpretation. We might not be able to agree as to where exactly the line should be drawn in our critical approach to the Bible and some might go too far, but one thing we do know: in the light of our modern understanding of science, the line cannot be drawn in such a way as to include the literal interpretation of Genesis. Fundamentalists are well-meaning, but I believe misguided, in presenting the issues in such a way as to imply that one must make a straight choice between two wholly incompatible viewpoints – the scientific and the religious. In so doing, they alienate those who would seek an honest reconciliation between their religious beliefs and their knowledge of modern science. In the process, the fundamentalists deny themselves, and others, the satisfaction of understanding the way God actually does go about his creative work and they fail to appreciate how modern science can throw new light on ancient truths – like the truth of original sin.

Before leaving this discussion of our instinctive behaviour, there is one further point I should add. I am sometimes asked why religious behaviour, like the other types of behaviour we have mentioned, should not be similarly regarded as no more than a response to some unconscious instinctive drive. After all, religious awareness is as universal among men as the mental attitudes we now attribute to instinct; moreover, the 'religious instinct' could have served a useful survival function through binding a community together against a common enemy. In answer, I would say first that I would be disturbed if religious awareness were *not* a universal manifestation. Had the phenomenon of religion emerged from a single tribe at a single point in time, it would have led to the suspicion that it was merely a cultural invention; God must surely relate to all men at all times. But the real flaw in this type of argument against religion can be seen when one examines the actual nature of a religion, particularly that of Christianity, and the effect that if has on the behaviour of its adherents. Any primitive animal unfortunate enough to suffer a mistake in its DNA copying such that the scrambled-up code gave rise to the message 'Love your enemies' would have been promptly eliminated by those enemies! No, an instinctive message of that kind could not have been perpetuated in the jungle-like conditions surrounding the emergence of man. The whole tenor of religious awareness and the behaviour to which it leads runs counter to the evolutionary drive towards self-survival, and so cannot be regarded as one of the surviving inherited instincts.

The support lent by the theory of evolution to the underlying assertion of the Adam and Eve story is not the only scientific evidence for the myth. At the end of the previous chapter, I mentioned that there had been not one, but two developments that had a bearing on the subject. Though there is still much more I want to say about the significance of the theory of evolution for religious belief, I propose we interrupt our discussion of that topic for a moment and take a brief look at this other development.

It arises in a field of investigation that is increasingly coming to be recognized as scientific in its approach – psychology. To see how psychology can provide insight into the nature of original sin, I want you to journey backwards in time and imagine yourself once again as a baby. As such, you have certain needs: you get hungry, and cold, and wet. What do you do about it? There is little you can do, except yell. After a few tries at this you discover that in response to persistent crying, one of those shadowy shapes out there in the surrounding world (probably the one you will later call 'mother') comes and feeds you, puts a blanket on you, or changes your nappy. This pattern of events repeats itself consistently, day in, day out. Clearly this is what those people out there are meant for; they exist to attend to your needs.

All very natural, you say; what is the problem? The problem is this: modern psychology has revealed the extraordinary importance of the first few years of life in forming our attitudes and shaping our characters. Those early years you spent as a baby were crucial for determining the kind of person you were later to become. Indeed, some psychologists would claim that mentally and emotionally you were even affected by events that occurred whilst you were still in your mother's womb. Be that as it may, one thing is certain; during the most significant, impressionable period of your life, you were being indoctrinated into thinking that the world revolved around you, people existed solely to attend to your needs and if you wanted anything you had only to yell for it. In other words, you daily had instilled into you an attitude of mind which, however natural and acceptable it might be in a baby, is one that is entirely anti-social if carried over into adulthood; it is an outlook that is self-centred and lacking in sensitivity towards the needs of others. There is no escaping this conditioning we receive as a baby; all of us, of necessity, are shaped in the same mould and begin our lives believing that we occupy the centre of life's stage.

Once again, but now from a completely different angle to that of evolution, we see that we become subject to a bias that makes us put our own self-interest first. Again, the source of the bias lies in the past; not this time in the distant past occupied by our primitive ancestors, but in our own early childhood. Thus, whether we are thinking of inherited tendencies or of those acquired in babyhood, the conclusion is the same: for reasons that lie beyond our control, there is something deep inside us which ensures that we fall short of our potential for good. And this, as we have seen, is the kernel of the Adam and Eve story.

All rather depressing, you might think. No wonder many gain the impression that religious belief is primarily concerned with confessing sin and being oppressed by feelings of guilt! But this is unfair. Though it is true that without help we are unable to do anything about our sinful tendencies, that is not the end of the matter. There is a source of external help: God. As we have seen from the creation myths, God is the embodiment of goodness and love. Having realistically faced up to what is wrong and unsatisfactory with our lives, we now know what has to be done to put things right; somehow or other, we must shift the focus of our attention away from self and re-centre our lives upon God. Any change less radical will not suffice. The confident, and ultimately optimistic, claim of religious belief – whether it be of Jew, Christian, or Moslem – is that, with God's help, this can be achieved.

6 The Emergence of the Human Spirit

If, as seems to be established by the theory of evolution, we are descended from the same ancestors as the apes, how is it that, alone among the animals, we are supposed to have a spirit?

A difficult question – one for which the answer is far from obvious. In fact, I have searched through quite a number of theological books and none, to my mind, comes up with a satisfactory explanation; indeed most simply ignore the issue. The neglect of such a central problem strikes me as odd. Could it be that Christians are reluctant to face up to the possibility that evolution has shown man not to be as unique as customarily thought?

Traditional Christian belief is quite clear in its assertion that man alone among creatures possesses an immortal spirit. It is the quality that places him in his special relationship with God. (Incidentally, in order to avoid confusion, I should perhaps point out that one often hears this quality referred to as the 'soul'. Strictly speaking this is incorrect; the word 'soul' ought to be reserved for something more closely akin to 'mind' – a property possessed by all animals.) But Darwin's theory appears to pose problems for this view of man's uniqueness. If man has an immortal spiritual dimension to life, why haven't the other animals the same? Man, after all, in evolutionary terms is just a highly developed animal. Though the gulf separating us from the apes or from other intelligent forms of life would seem to be large, it is now recognized as being a difference of degree rather than of kind. Moreover, if one imagines progressively going back in time, it is a gulf that narrows; our own ancestors and those of the apes become more and more similar until a point is reached, a few million years ago, where the two lines of development merge into one.

So the problem of how we, and not the apes, could come to have spirits is a real one. Are we to believe that at some arbitrary point on this smooth gradation, God decided to declare officially that man had arrived and proceeded to introduce a spirit into each member of one generation whilst denying it to members of the previous one – despite the fact that because of the random variations between individuals, some members of the older generation might be considered more 'advanced' than others of the new generation? That is a scenario that certainly has little appeal for me. Though, of course, I have no way of knowing for sure what really did happen, I nevertheless feel compelled as a Christian to offer at least some plausible scheme as to what *might* have occurred. To this end, I suggest the following.

The prime concern in the early stages of evolution was with survival – the need simply to stay alive. Then at a certain stage in the development of man, his intelligence reached a level at which thoughts began to reach out beyond the immediate needs of food, sex, comfort and security, to questions about existence: why he was here and what purpose there might be to life. At this point in human history, there emerged a potential for discerning a divine presence. At first, there was only the merest hint of this capability, but with succeeding generations it grew and deepened. A nebulous, hesitant response was evoked and, imperceptibly, a wordless communion with God commenced. With the coming of speech, probably no more than 50,000 years ago, there came a great upsurge of understanding of all kinds. Suddenly each individual's perception became widened. No longer confined to the knowledge his own personal experience of life had taught him, he was now able to gain access to the knowledge and wisdom gained through the lives of others. A vast fund of shared knowledge became available to all, providing insights both into the working of nature and into diverse experiences of God. Speech also brought with it the articulation of thought – the possibility of developing rich and complex trains of intricate thought. With speech, for the first time a dialogue with God could be established.

Thus, I suggest, the evolution of our physical bodies was accom-

33

panied by an evolution of the spirit. No sharp dividing line would have separated those animals possessing spirits from those that did not. Primitive man would have been endowed with a primitive spirit. As for what I mean by a 'primitive spirit', let me try to explain with an analogy. Imagine two people going to a symphony concert. For one, it is his first experience of listening to Beethoven. Brought up on a diet of pop music, the concert means little to him; he finds it tedious and boring, apart from one or two brief passages where he thought he could detect a tune of sorts. His companion on the other hand, himself a professional musician, is quite carried away; not only is the symphony well known to him and much loved, but from his own experience of taking part in performances of it, he recognizes this to be the performance of a lifetime – one remarkable for the conductor's sensitivity and for the subtlety of the instrumental playing. Two listeners then, but the same concert – one listener able to appreciate the concert just a little, the other a great deal. So I would think it is with our spirits. There can be two spirits in communion with the same God giving rise to responses altogether different in their intensity and richness. Whilst both spirits would possess in equal measure the quality of immortality, the primitive one, characteristic of an early ancestor of ours, would be operating at a lower level of awareness compared to the more fully developed one belonging to modern man; one of them would find heaven no more than mildly diverting, whilst to the other it would be a place of great wonder and joy.

And just as I would not draw a sharp distinction between modern man and the ancestors that preceded him, I would not make a hard and fast distinction between him and the other animals existing today. To the extent that some animals might have the power to grasp some rudimentary thought on the possible existence of God and could respond with love, then I see nothing wrong in believing such animals to have some rudimentary form of spirit. It would not surprise me to learn that St Peter's gates are kept ajar for the odd dog or dolphin to squeeze in!

There is, of course, no evidence I can point to in support of the above ideas; they are speculative and I do not expect you necessarily to go along with them. The reason for advancing them is merely to illustrate that there is at least one way in which the basic tenets of

Christian belief concerning the spirit could be modified in, I believe, an inessential way, to bring them into harmony with the theory of evolution.

7 Superhuman Life-forms?

The theory of evolution poses questions not only to do with our past ancestors, but also, in the opposite direction along the time-scale, in regard to there being life-forms possibly more advanced than man. Evolution, as we have already noted, is still taking place in our own times, so it is interesting to reflect on what life-forms might develop a million or ten million years from now. And if man is to be regarded as a mere staging-post along the way towards some more advanced creature, ought we not to ask why Jesus chose to come into the world as a man rather than wait until he could come in a superior form. Indeed, might it not be that more advanced forms of life exist on other planets in the universe already? How is Jesus supposed to relate to *them*?

To put such questions into perspective, we first enquire how likely it is for there to be extra-terrestrial life-forms, and secondly, how long it takes for radically superior life-forms to develop.

We begin by noting the breath-taking array of stars revealed by the modern astronomical telescope. Our sun is but one of many that make up a group of stars called a galaxy. The number of those stars is 100,000 million. To gain some appreciation of the magnitude of such a number, suppose that a close-up photograph of each star has been taken and you want to examine it for evidence as to whether the star is accompanied by a planet supporting life. You allow yourself just one second to study each star. How long will it take? The answer is that you (or more accurately, your descendants) would still be at it after 3,000 years! And that is only the beginning. Our galaxy is not alone; there are 100,000 million of them. So, the examination of the photographs would take 3,000 years even if you were to devote only one second to each entire galaxy, rather than one second to each star.

All stars having presumably formed in much the same way as our own sun, that is from the condensation of swirling gas, it cannot be doubted that a proportion of them will also have planets around them. Though the majority of these might be similar to Mercury, Venus, Mars, Saturn and Jupiter, with conditions hostile to the development of life, one can hardly doubt that many of them will be as suitable for supporting life as our earth. The chances of a star having a planet capable of supporting life are thought to lie somewhere between one-in-ten and one-in-a-thousand. Though this cannot be anything other than a crude estimate, even were it to be out by a factor of a million (or a billion!) it would still leave a vast number of potential life-bearing homes.

This being so, it is only reasonable to suppose that life has indeed evolved elsewhere in the universe. The course of evolution would have proceeded independently on each planet and, at any instant of time, would have been either more, or less, advanced in one place than in another. Creatures that were recognizably man developed here on earth a few million years ago. Though this is a long time as judged by every-day standards, on the evolutionary time-scale it is not. If we were to imagine the whole of earth's history compressed into the space of one year, man would have been around for only a few hours; he comes onto the scene late in the evening of the 31st December. It follows that the evolutionary process on some other planet does not have to get very far out of step with that on earth for it to have either no creatures the equal of man, or alternatively much more advanced ones. Who can say, for instance, what creatures exist there now, if, on the compressed time-scale, the equivalent of man emerged in the morning of 31st December rather than in the evening?

As for the future development of life here on earth, it is anybody's guess as to what lies in store. It would be difficult enough to make a prediction were the process of evolution to carry on in the same random fashion as it has in the past. But now a new feature must be included in the reckoning. For the first time on earth, a species has emerged that is consciously aware of the process of evolution and, moreover, under-stands the mechanism by which inherited characteristics are passed

37

on from one generation to another. This knowledge could, in time, lead to an ability to *control* the direction evolution takes and the pace at which it advances. Such control is already being exercised to a limited extent and could be further applied in a number of ways. These include: genetic counselling on the risks of certain couples having deformed children; the early detection and abortion of abnormal embryos; artificial insemination leading to the enhancement of some chosen donors' characteristics (however the choice might be made); clonal reproduction, whereby the nucleus of a body cell is placed into the egg of another, the original nucleus of which has been removed, thus leading to the production of offspring that are genetically the same as the donor of the nucleus (a technique for producing an unlimited number of identical Einsteins, for example); and molecular engineering where one tampers with the DNA codes themselves. Though some of these possibilities are not regarded as socially acceptable, it would be unwise to assume that this will always remain the case. Certainly if man did decide to apply seriously his growing knowledge of genetics, he could cause an unprecedented acceleration to the evolutionary process.

In summary, these various conjectures lead us to the real possibility that one day there might exist on earth a life-form that is greatly in advance of our own – a superior life-form, equivalent to others that might exist elsewhere in the universe already. This being the case, we are prompted to ask how such speculations affect the Bible's assessment of we who exist here and now.

My own feeling is that it makes very little difference. Though I have argued that a certain degree of intelligence is required to reach the point where one can begin to question the purpose of life and so enter into a relationship with God, that does not mean that there has to be an exact correlation between intellectual and spiritual capacity. Once a certain minimum level of intellectual development has been reached, I suspect there is little, if any, further correspondence between the two. After all, it is known from experience that among the most profoundly religious and deeply spiritual people are to be found unlearned and simple folk as well as geniuses and scholars. Christianity had need of the fisherman, Peter, as well as the intellectual, Paul. Equating wisdom with knowledge or cleverness is a mistake; cerebral giants can be spiritual pygmies. So the higher life-forms we have been contemplating, whilst possessing greater intelligence, need not have a greater spiritual capability than ourselves. Though man could be comparatively low down in the universe's intellectual pecking order, he might figure differently on that other evolutionary ladder we discussed: the parallel development leading to the spirit.

In support of this view, we note that Jesus once said, and was himself to demonstrate, that there was no greater love than that a man should lay down his life for another; it is the ultimate expression of love. Man has reached that stage in his spiritual development where he can so commit himself to God that he is willing to make this supreme sacrifice if and when it is required of him. Such a level of commitment can be bettered neither here on earth by some future life-form nor on any other planet in the universe. Because it is the quality of our love for God which determines the depth of our spiritual nature, I believe the Bible is not so very far from the mark in its assessment of the stature of man. In matters relating to the immortal spirit, he might well have his equal elsewhere, but is unlikely to have a superior.

Turning to the question of how Jesus relates to life-forms elsewhere in the universe, the Christian belief, as we shall discuss in detail in chapter 18, is that in Jesus we see the eternal omnipresent Son of God identifying himself with humanity. To do this he took on the form of a man and subjected himself to the same restrictions regarding space and time as apply to ourselves; he entered the world at a particular point in space and time. This being so, I see no reason why the same Son of God should not also have identified himself with other forms of life at other times and in other places in the universe. If life has evolved on other planets according to the same principle of natural selection as holds on earth, creatures there will show the same marks of original sin and so will be as much in need of him as we are.

With regard to why the Son of God came to earth at the particular time he did, this is something where one just cannot win. Regardless of when he came, someone is bound to ask: Why then? The time actually chosen was quite propitious. It needed to be reasonably early in the development of mankind so that most of us could live our lives in the knowledge of him. But it would have been useless his coming before that knowledge could become widespread and could endure into succeeding generations. The development of speech would, therefore, be an obvious prerequisite. But that by itself would have been inadequate; there needed, in addition, to be good communications by road and sea so that the gospel could be widely disseminated from one country to another. All in all, it can be argued that the era of the Roman Empire was probably the most effective point in time for Jesus to make his appearance and that is indeed when he did come.

In response to the question as to why the Son of God did not delay his coming until some higher life-form than man had evolved, I have already indicated an answer: the higher life-form whilst having a greater intelligence, would not necessarily possess a greater spiritual capacity. There is, however, another reason. It is a disturbing one, but one that ought, nevertheless, to be faced; the possibility of nuclear annihilation. The emergence of man might well mark the end of the evolutionary process; there might not be any forms of life higher than man.

Reflect for a moment on the uniqueness of the present time in the history of life on earth. The progress of evolution up to this point has been characterized by unremitting ruthlessness and violence. Man's ancestors were not particularly well-favoured for the struggle in regard to strength, or speed, or natural weapons such as claws and strong teeth, or protection through a tough hide or shell. Their advantage lay in their intelligence. This allowed them to supplement their modest physical attributes through the use of objects they found or could make; at first, stones and sticks; then spears and arrows; and later guns, ships, tanks, aircraft and missiles. At each stage they did not hesitate to use whatever came to hand; not only did they have the cleverness and manual dexterity to construct weapons, but also, it appears, an instinctive will to put them to use. This self-seeking, aggressive trait, so essential to survival in the past, seems, as we have noted earlier, to be eradicably etched into the fabric of our bodies (in the form of the DNA molecules) and thereby into our mental make-up. It is the fact that man now, for the first time, has a weapon sufficiently powerful to destroy the whole human race, that accords our point in history its unique quality. The question to my mind is not 'Will he use this power to destroy himself completely?', but '*When* will he use it?'

Whilst speaking in this vein to a gathering of school-children in Jersey a few years ago, I found my comments greeted by stunned disbelief and dismay. I shall not easily forget their reaction. I quickly tried to reassure them that nuclear annihilation was probably a long way off and their chances of being victims of it were probably less than the likelihood of their being knocked down in a car accident that day. But this did little to set their minds at rest. So, recalling that experience, let me be clear about the nature of my admittedly rather pessimistic forecast.

In the first few years after the development of nuclear weapons and the onset of the nuclear arms race, the chance of an immediate global catastrophe was, by common consent, high. We all held our breath over the Hungarian and Czechoslovak crises, the Berlin air-lift and the attempt to ship Russian missiles to Cuba. But we survived. Not even full-scale wars like that in Vietnam have led to the use of nuclear weapons. As each uneasy year goes by, it can be argued that the nations are becoming more accustomed to the new rules of the game under which power struggles have to be conducted if catastrophe is to be avoided. Despite the sheer immensity of the ever-accumulating stockpiles of nuclear war-heads, an increasing source of anxiety, I am more confident now than at any previous time that my own generation will be able to live out its days in comparative peace and that my children and grandchildren will also succeed in averting nuclear disaster. Indeed I hope mankind will continue along this path for a hundred years, five hundred years, or, who knows, perhaps even a thousand years.

But, in the context of evolutionary change, such periods are as nothing. On the compressed time-scale described earlier, where man emerged a few hours before midnight on the 31st December, a further thousand years would be equivalent to taking us into the New Year by a few seconds. One kiss under the mistletoe and that is all. So although we ourselves might not be directly affected in the final holocaust, the outlook for mankind in general is bleak. I find this conclusion inescapable. Can anyone seriously claim that over the next few thousand years no unbalanced dictator, like Hitler, will rise to power in a country with a nuclear capability, or that no nuclear war will be triggered off by human or computer error? Someday it *has* to happen and when it does, that will be the end of the evolutionary process on earth. Though some primitive forms of life, such as bacteria, would in all probability survive, advanced forms will not.

As far as life on earth is concerned, therefore, I find myself led to the conclusion that present-day man essentially represents the highest form of life there is ever likely to be. This being so, further point is given to Jesus having come at the time in history that he did.

What of the ultimate fate of life elsewhere? I expect the same story in its important elements to be repeated. Life will have evolved on other planets in the same harsh way as it did on earth. Though it is of interest to try and think of some process that is more benign than that which characterized terrestrial evolution, I have not myself succeeded in finding one. For there to be evolutionary development, there has to be selection; selection implies not only winners but losers – the fortunate survive whilst the less-favoured are eliminated. So, from essentially the same process of evolution by natural selection as we have on earth, I expect animals the equal of man in regard to intelligence to have emerged on other planets. They almost certainly will not look anything like us; they might, for example, have eyes in the back of their head (a useful survival feature). But, regardless of how different they might look, they will share with us an equivalent intellectual capacity – an ability that will lead them not only to the discovery of God, but also to the discovery of nuclear power. Being subject to the same instinctive drives as ourselves – so essential to survival in the early stages of evolution, but ultimately so destructive – they will then be set to follow the same course as ourselves.

In the face of such an outlook, some people find it hard to believe there can be any real purpose to life. In particular, they question how any God could have set in motion a train of events destined to end so disastrously. It all seems so pointless.

The answer has to do with one's perspective. In the first place, there is a need to recognize that intelligent life on earth was due to come to an end in any case, even without the assistance of nuclear war. Life on earth exists because the conditions here are favourable. But these will not always remain so. The sun, which so intimately governs the terrestrial environment, is itself evolving. There will come a time, millions of years from now, when conditions on earth will have so changed that they will no longer be capable of sustaining life. Indeed, all life throughout the universe is destined to come to an end one day. In due course stars expand in size, engulfing their nearby planets in flames (the expected fate of earth), and finally exhaust their fuel leaving any remaining planets cold and lifeless. So, in a sense, nuclear annihilation merely brings forward in time something that has to happen anyway. Secondly, we must not overlook the fact that what we are talking about here is the fate of mankind in general (and of similar species on other planets); nothing we have said need have any direct bearing upon you, or me, or any other individual. We all have to die sometime; that much has not changed. To the individual, it is of little consequence whether his own death is an isolated incident, or whether he is one among many casualties in a war, or in the final holocaust. From the individual's point of view, there might, indeed, be much to be said for a quick death from a direct hit by a nuclear bomb than a slow one on the end of a conventional bayonet. In the final analysis, each of us is faced with the fact of our own mortality and that is the way it has always been – nuclear weapons or no nuclear weapons.

But, in regard to this matter of keeping things in perspective, the most important point of all to a Christian, and to many another religious believer, is the recognition that the life we live here on earth is not in any case meant to be an end in itself. God's prime purpose in creating the world was not to have life crawling on its planets in perpetuity. The intention was to bring into existence spiritual creatures that could develop a loving relationship with him. Though the fashioning of these spiritual beings is through the medium of physical bodies operating in a physical world, it is not the physical that is significant. The physical is merely the means to the end. Once the immortal spirit has come to full-flower and is capable of independent existence, the physical life that gave birth to it becomes expendable. The Christian perspective is one in which human spirits are continually being harvested. Whether a large number are gathered in on a single occasion through some calamity, or progressively through natural mortality, has little significance. Nor does it matter that one day the earth is destined to return to its former desolate condition through nuclear war or otherwise; the final state of the earth in no way diminishes the value of the life it once bore. Our planet would have played its part in contributing to the spiritual harvest and it is the fruits of that harvest which endure.

8 Miracles Under Scrutiny

Turning aside from evolution and its various implications, let us now take a look at a different topic: miracles. It is a subject that figures in discussions of science and religion with almost as much regularity as evolution and it is not difficult to see why: if the scientist's job is to uphold the laws of nature, how can he have anything to do with supposed violations of those laws? Doesn't modern science tell us that miracles just do not happen?

From the outset, I should perhaps mention that my use of the word 'miracle', will be quite specific: it will refer to an interruption to the normal workings of nature – a violation of a scientific law. This is not always the meaning it carries in common usage. A newspaper describing an aircraft crash-landing without loss of life might carry a headline 'Miracle Escape'. Although the circumstances of the incident might be remarkable, so remarkable as to lead some to believe that God's protection had been at work, no miracle, in the sense that I shall be using the term, need have occurred.

The question of whether the laws of nature can actually be broken is for us an obvious one to ask. For the early church it was not. Prior to the development of science, many happenings lacked explanation – not only those we today would regard as miraculous. The examination of miracle stories in those days was concerned not so much with whether the incident had occurred, but rather with the underlying intention of the story. Did it have an inner meaning? Did it convey spiritual insight into the nature of God? Such a study could be carried on independently of the story having, in addition, a basis in historical fact – a point we shall need to remember in our own investigation of miracle stories.

Concern for historicity began to stir only later. This came about through contact with Greek philosophical thought based on the harmonious working of nature. With the growth of science, the requirement that nature behaves in an orderly, predictable manner became more insistent. By the seventeenth century, the climate of secular opinion had become distinctly hostile to the notion that the regular operation of the newly formulated laws of physics should be regarded as subject to erratic supernaturalistic intervention.

Paradoxically, Christian thinking had meanwhile moved in the opposite direction; it had come increasingly to rely on the historical truth of miracles. One reason for this was the effect we have already noted: the tendency in the post-Reformation period to accord all biblical writings – not just miracle stories – a literal interpretation. A second was associated with wider travel, a greater number of people finding opportunities to journey abroad and learn of other cultures. One outcome was an increased awareness of the diversity of world religions; Christianity was not alone. How then was it still to be regarded as unique? The answer lay in the conviction that Jesus was the Son of God. But how was this assertion to be proved? Miracles appeared to provide the solution: Jesus' ability to perform them was evidence of his divine nature. Thus ever greater dependence came to be invested in the historical accuracy of miracle stories – at a time when the movement of secular thought made such belief increasingly harder to sustain. The result was confusion. It is that confusion we must now endeavour to resolve.

But, before we begin, perhaps a disclaimer would be in order. As a scientist, I do not have any special right to pronounce on whether miracles do or do not happen. True, it is my task to investigate the workings of nature and help formulate the laws governing its behaviour. But these laws refer only to the normal habitual working of nature. Miracles, as we have said, refer to behaviour that is out of the ordinary. Whether the laws are sometimes violated in this way, I am no more qualified to say than you. The most that I and my fellow scientists can claim is that, through our long and careful study of the laws in action, we are better placed than most to appreciate the consistency with which they are generally obeyed; they are rules of behaviour not to be set aside lightly.

The miracle stories are a mixed bag. There can be no easy answer, 'Yes, I believe them', or 'No, I do not believe them'. Each must be treated on its own merits. We must enquire not only into the circumstances surrounding the individual story, but also into prevailing attitudes towards miracle stories in general and into the nature and character of such narrations in ancient literature. Our approach must be systematic.

We begin by enquiring what Jesus' own professed attitude was towards the performance of miracles. From a study of his temptations in the wilderness we find that, rather like a scientist, he, too, had respect for the laws of nature. He was much concerned with the right and wrong use of miraculous power. He wondered at one stage, for example, whether he should use it to impress people by throwing himself off buildings without getting hurt. Such displays of supernatural power would undoubtedly have drawn attention to himself and convinced people that he came from God. But that, he decided was not the point. His purpose in coming into the world was to show God's love for man and to evoke in his hearers a responding love. For this response to be genuine it had to be freely offered; it had not to arise from coercion or fear. For this reason he decided against spectacular miracles performed for their own sake.

This rule of action was one he was to reiterate on more than one occasion. When the scribes and Pharisees asked for a sign, he rejected the request with the words: 'It is an evil and unfaithful generation that asks for a sign!' Referring to the ancient myth of Jonah, Jesus declared that the only signs he would give were those of his resurrection (his three-day stay in the tomb being paralleled by Jonah's sojourn in the belly of the sea-monster) and his preaching (the power of his own preaching being compared to that of Jonah to the citizens of Nineveh). The fruitlessness of performing miracles is again stated in Jesus' story of the rich man and the beggar Lazarus. In torment in Hades, the rich man appeals to Abraham to allow Lazarus to return to warn his brothers to repent and thus avoid a similar fate. Abraham replies, 'If they will not listen either to Moses or to the prophets, they will not be convinced even if someone should rise from the dead.' These declarations by Jesus, that he would not perform gratuitous miracles in order to conform people into believing in him, provide a background against which we must make our judgments.

In tackling any individual miracle story, the first point to establish is the prior one of whether there was in fact anything essentially miraculous about the event described. Could there not have been a natural explanation of the phenomenon?

A particularly good example of a miracle story that has arisen from a perfectly normal occurrence is to be found in the Old Testament: Moses feeding the Israelite people in the desert on manna and quails. Manna is now recognized to be nothing more remarkable than a secretion given out by certain insects (*Trabutina mannipara*) on tamarisk leaves. This occurs between May and July. It comes in the form of pale yellow, syrupy drops, the size of peas. They fall to the ground towards morning and are gathered by Bedouin. As for the quails accompanying the manna, their sudden appearance also has a simple explanation – great flocks of them regularly migrate from Africa across Egypt and Palestine in the spring; some become tired by their long journey, fall to the ground and are then easily caught.

Certain of the miracles attributed to Jesus also lend themselves to naturalistic explanation. With our greater understanding of the working of the mind and its effects on bodily health, today we would class some of the healing miracles as the work of a good psychiatrist, rather than a miracle worker. These would include the 'casting out of devils' and the cure of other ailments that could have been of psychosomatic origin.

But not many of the miracle stories yield easily to naturalistic interpretations. Dogged adherence to this approach rapidly degenerates into bizarre speculation. Jesus' walking on the water, for instance, has been variously ascribed to his wading in shallow water (despite the boat carrying the disciples being three or four miles from land) and to his standing on a floating log of wood. Even more contrived are theories based on the premise that Jesus, in addition to his regular disciples, had a band of under-cover agents whose job was to help 'stage' the miracles. Prior to Jesus' preaching in the wilderness, for example, they saw to it that a nearby cave was well-stocked with loaves and fishes ready for the miraculous feeding of the multitude. Despite their implausibility, theories such as these managed to attract some attention in the eighteenth century, but I do not think they need detain us.

The next way of accounting for miracles is what we might call the pseudo-naturalistic approach. According to this, miracles are regarded not so much as being contrary to nature but rather as an acceleration of a natural process. St Augustine was one accustomed to arguing in this vein. In respect of the feeding of the multitude he had this to say:

> For whence came so great a quantity of food to fill so many thousands? The source of the bread was in the hands of the Lord. That need not surprise us. For he that made from five loaves bread to fill so many thousands was the same who daily prepares mighty harvests in the earth from but a few grains.

Likewise, he would reason that, in the normal course of events, water, in the form of rain water, was turned into wine, God using the vine as an intermediary. Jesus, in turning water into wine at the marriage-feast at Cana, was merely hastening this process.

There is no doubt that this argument has a certain appeal: it makes miracles seem more acceptable. Natural processes can indeed be accelerated (the reaction between two chemicals in a test-tube, for example, often is speeded up by a rise in temperature). But that hardly alters the fact that the occurrences reported in the miracle stories were not simply the normal processes happening more quickly than usual; they were *different* processes. Bread comes from wheat grain as Augustine says, but in the feeding of the multitude the extra bread came from bread. The production of wine certainly requires water, but it requires other chemicals as well and these do not appear to have been to hand when Jesus performed the miracle at Cana. No, this superficially attractive idea for playing down the unnaturalness of miracles will not do. The majority of miracle stories present us with a claim which – if accepted at face-value – means nothing less than that something has happened contrary to the natural order.

That being the case, the next question to ask is whether the miracle story might have been generated, quite innocently, through a misunderstanding of some kind. After all, the gospel accounts were not written by eye-witnesses, neither were they recorded immediately after the events described. In the telling and re-telling of the stories, a misconception might have crept in – one that had the effect of converting an ordinary story into one purporting to describe a miracle.

49

At least one of Jesus' miracles succumbs to this interpretation: his walking on the water. You will recall how the disciples were in a fishing boat on the Lake of Galilee when, in the distance, they saw Jesus walking on the water. Peter, who is known to have been rather impetuous, gets out of the boat in order to go to him; he tries walking but ends up floundering.

Considered in isolation it is difficult to know what to make of the account. There seems little point to the miracle; indeed, it rather smacks of a display of supernatural power for its own sake. Having in the wilderness rejected as a cheap trick the idea of defying gravity by throwing himself off a building, can we be happy about his motive for defying gravity by walking on the water? The suspicion that all is not well with this miracle story is confirmed when one views it not in isolation, but alongside a somewhat similar story.

This second story concerns an occasion soon after Jesus' resurrection. The disciples were once again in a boat on the Lake of Galilee. They now see Jesus on the seashore. Peter, impatient as ever, cannot wait for the boat to be rowed ashore and instead jumps out of it, presumably to swim to Jesus.

The two stories are similar, the only significant difference being that in one, Jesus is walking on the sea, whereas in the other he is walking on the seashore. It is at this point that biblical scholars have something interesting to contribute. Among the various techniques they have devised for examining the Bible, is one in which they trace the accounts back to their earliest versions written in the original language. This can sometimes reveal mistranslations or nuances of meaning that were possessed by the original and were subsequently lost. This approach, when applied to our two stories, comes up with a remarkable discovery. The scholars have uncovered an ambiguity of meaning: the original Greek phrase for 'on the sea' had an alternative meaning, 'on the seashore'. It immediately becomes clear what, in all likelihood has happened. Our two stories derive from a single original one. In the retelling of that story someone got hold of the wrong end of the stick and inadvertently created the miracle story. Further reason for believing this to be the explanation comes from the statement attributed to the disciples when they saw Jesus walking on the sea; they are reported to have said: 'It is a ghost'. This does not fit altogether easily into the miracle story but is exactly what the disciples are likely to have concluded on being confronted with Jesus walking on the seashore a few days after they had witnessed his death.

In this example, a probable source of error is clearly pin-pointed. But in addition to this kind of mistake – one specific to a particular story – we have to contend with a potentially much more serious source of misunderstanding. It was one capable of spawning not just one spurious miracle story, but several. It arose from the Jewish expectation of a Messiah: 'Yahweh your God will raise up for you a prophet like myself, from among yourselves.' This prophecy by the dying Moses led the Jewish people to look for the coming of a Messiah. Just as Moses had delivered his people from the rule of the Egyptians, so the Messiah would also be a great deliverer; as Moses had performed miracles, so, too, would the Messiah. That was the expectation. The realization that Jesus was that long-awaited Messiah came to the disciples but slowly. This was understandable – in certain ways, he was not what they had been led to expect. Instead of a political figure leading his people against the Roman oppressors, he came preaching love and reconciliation. Instead of victory in battle, he allowed himself to be crucified. This, as we now understand, was because Jesus came to fulfil not only Moses' prophecy concerning the Messiah, but also that of Isaiah concerning the 'suffering servant' – an enigmatic figure who was in some sense or other to become a sacrifice for the sins of mankind. Until the time of Jesus, no one had really understood this latter prophecy – and certainly no one had made the connection between the two prophecies and realized that they referred to one and the same person. Accordingly, the Jewish people's interpretation of the nature of the messiahship was not that of Jesus.

As the true significance of Jesus' mission came to be appreciated by his disciples, they began to spread the word that he was the Messiah. This bold assertion was bound to cause misunderstanding. The hearers of the message would automatically infer that all the traditional expectations of the Messiah had been fulfilled – including those relating to the miracles. As Moses had fed the multitude in the desert, so presumably Jesus had fed a multitude in a desert. As Moses had commanded the sea to obey him (when he took the Israelites across the Red Sea), so presumably Jesus must have commanded a sea to obey him (the stilling of the storm on the Lake of Galilee). How else, so it would be argued, would Jesus' disciples have known that their master was the Messiah unless it had been through the giving of the looked-for signs?

Thus, we can see how, in that vital period during which people were having to adjust their thinking to this new conception of messiahship, rumours would have started circulating. A process would have been set in motion whereby, in effect, the ancient miracle stories associated with Moses would have been transposed in time and attached, in some variant or other, to the growing tradition surrounding the person of Jesus. Given the prevailing mood of the times, according to which unashamed delight was taken in accounts of miracles and wondrous happenings, it was almost bound to happen.

That last remark introduces a new and important aspect of our discussion: the prevailing mood of the times. How *did* people in those days feel about miracle stories? The fact that we ourselves incline towards scepticism, should not lead us to assume that they did also – we have been exposed to scientific thought in our up-bringing, they had not. In fact, the evidence is that they thought about such matters in a radically different way from ourselves. This is most clearly to be seen in a number of documents that circulated freely in the days of the early church, but which have since sunk into obscurity.

Among the stories they contained are some that supposedly fill in the details on Jesus' childhood – the period from his birth to his first appearance in the temple. We read, for instance, that Jesus used to make clay models of birds – which promptly flew away. One day a boy accidentally ran into him; Jesus cursed him and he fell down dead. One of the swaddling bands, taken by the wise men as a memento of their visit to the infant Jesus, was thrown onto a fire, but would not burn. Children with leprosy, on being bathed in the same water as that used to wash Jesus, were instantly cured. A young man who had been turned into a mule by witchcraft was restored through Mary placing Jesus on his back. These and other fantastic stories are to be found in documents such as 'The Infancy Gospel of Thomas' and 'The Arabic Gospel of the Childhood'.

Likewise, there circulated stories about the apostles. We read, for instance, how they were constantly raising people from the dead. On one occasion, Peter converted a large number of bystanders by throwing a kipper into water and bringing it back to life. He had conversations with a dog, the animal replying with a human voice. A magician, in the course of a contest with Peter, levitated himself to a great height above the town; Peter pointed out to God that this feat was not doing the Christian cause any good; God thereupon nullified the evil power and caused the magician to fall back to earth breaking his leg in three places. The story ends happily with the on-lookers stoning the poor fellow to death and declaring themselves converts to Christianity! These are but a selection of the incidents described in The Acts of Peter, The Acts of John, The Gospel of Peter and a host of similar books.

Collectively, these documents, written mostly in the second century, are known as the New Testament Apocrypha. They were excluded from the canon of the New Testament (that is to say, from the list of books that comprise the New Testament). It is not difficult to see why: much of what they contained was clearly blatant invention. But although we might regard such writings with amusement today, they do have an important and serious significance for us: they alert us to the fact that, around the time of Jesus and for a while afterwards, miracle stories were being generated, not only through innocent misunderstandings, but also quite deliberately. They were being created for readers who quite simply loved hearing about such things.

For us, concerned as we are with the historical truth of the biblical miracle stories, this realization raises an obvious and, to some, worrying query: could it be that the books *within* the Bible also contain miracle stories that have been deliberately invented?

Before we can hope to answer this question, we must first find out how our present-day Bible came into existence and what kind of relationship the canonical books have to the non-canonical ones.

The problem of which books to regard as holy scripture and which not, was the subject of centuries-long discussion and disagreement. Even the Old Testament did not assume its final form until AD 90 – and then it was accepted only by the Palestinian Jews, the Hellenistic Jews insisting on the inclusion of several additional books. The Christian community, for its own part, came to adopt the shorter version of the Old Testament and the extra books contained in the longer version were consigned to what is now known as the Apocrypha.

As for the New Testament, it was not until the end of the second century that the church even began to consider the possibility that there might be a companion volume to the Old Testament, one comprising selected documents relating to the life of Jesus and the beginnings of the early church, and that this too might be regarded as having the status of holy scripture. At first, this new list consisted solely of a multilated version of Luke's Gospel, together with ten of Paul's epistles. The collection then developed into the gospels of Mark, Matthew, Luke and John and thirteen epistles of Paul. Other documents were added later. By the early fourth century, the historian Bishop Eusebius had divided books into three main categories: (i) 'acknowledged' (these including the four gospels, the Acts of the Apostles, the epistles of Paul, the First Epistle of Peter and the First Epistle of John); (ii) 'disputed' (the epistles of James and Jude, the Second and Third Epistles of John, the Second Epistle of Peter and the Book of Revelation); and (iii) 'spurious' or 'heretical' (Acts of Paul, the Epistle of Barnabas, etc.). By AD 340 the list had become the same as our modern New Testament, with the exception of the Book of Revelation, this last book not gaining final acceptance until towards the end of the fourth century.

From this chequered history, we see that the early church had no clear and unambiguous way of deciding what constituted scripture and what did not. It was only with the passage of time that certain books emerged as having greater lasting value, others proving less helpful and falling into disuse. This is not to say that the books finally excluded from the canon were later considered to have no value at all. Some of them undoubtedly provide a record of genuine sayings and authentic details of the life of Jesus and a few continued in use in certain churches long after the canon was finalized. It was really a matter of weighing up the pros and cons. For some books, the balance came down on one side, and for the remainder, it came down on the other.

In the light of this, it is difficult to accept that the books eventually included in the Bible were of a totally different character to those excluded – superior, yes, and in some cases markedly so, but the difference is one of degree only. This is not a view all Christians would accept. In defence of their assertion that the books in the Bible are altogether different from those outside it, they speak of divine inspiration – the holy scriptures are inspired by God. According to one view of what this means, the Bible was actually dictated word for word by God. The role of the writers was merely that of mechanically setting the words down on paper. This interpretation of the term 'divine inspiration' has had a long tradition – it was, as we saw earlier, the view expressed by the Council of Trent in 1546. But, despite its long history, it has been an interpretation that has always had its difficulties. How are we to account, for example, for the manifest errors and inconsistencies, the grammatical mistakes and the changes in literary style as one goes from book to book? They seem impossible to reconcile with the idea of only one (infallible) author.

A less extreme understanding of what is meant by divine inspiration, and one towards which the Roman Catholic church has tended to move since the time of the Council of Trent, is that it is not the words directly that are inspired, but the writers; the authors wrote under the influence of God; God revealed himself to the writers and they had then to express that revelation in their writings. Thus, we find the 1965 Second Vatican Council speaking of writers working under the *inspiration* of the Holy Spirit rather than at his *dictation*. The Council decree went on to state:

... the interpreter of sacred Scripture, in order to see clearly what God wanted to communicate to us, should carefully investigate what meaning the sacred writers really intended, and what God wanted to manifest by means of their words.

It also recognized that the writers had their own purposes in writing – purposes distinct from the divine purpose. This second interpretation of the term divine inspiration seems much more acceptable to us in view of what we now know about the nature of the biblical writings and how the books of the Bible came to be chosen. It is an interpretation that allows other influences to be at work – including possibly, in the present context, the tendency for miracle stories to proliferate with time.

Evidence seemingly pointing to the conclusion that certain biblical

55

miracle stories have in fact been deliberately generated is to be found through a comparison of the ways Mark and Luke handle two particular incidents.

The first concerns Jesus' call to the fishermen, Simon, Andrew, James and John. In Mark's account, Jesus simply says to them, 'Follow me and I will make you into fishers of men'; they promptly leave their nets and follow him. In Luke's version, the same words are spoken, but only after there has been a miraculous haul of fish – a catch so great as to cause Peter to fall on his knees before Jesus, his companions also being 'completely overcome'. The miraculous element of the story only occurs in this latter account.

The second incident concerns the arrest of Jesus in the Garden of Gethsemane. In the ensuing scuffle, Mark describes how one of Jesus' followers cuts off the ear of the high priest's servant. That is all – the ear is simply cut off. In Luke's Gospel, however, the story once again acquires a miraculous twist: Jesus puts the ear back on and heals it.

Now, we can understand how an incident can appear in one gospel and not another; one of the writers might not have heard of that particular story, or otherwise chose not to include it in his narrative, perhaps because it did not fit in with the storyline he was developing. But, in these two examples, the writers were describing the *same* incidents. Moreover, they were ones purporting to involve *miracles*. And yet Mark describes the events in a purely matter-of-fact manner without any hint of a miracle having occurred. Why? The answer must surely be that in the intervening period between the writing of Mark's Gospel and that of Luke, the stories have been elaborated. Perhaps Luke himself was responsible for the transformation; possibly the stories had already acquired their new dimension before being related to Luke.

Further evidence suggesting the accretion of miracle stories comes from a comparison of all four gospels and the writings of Paul. Paul's epistles are the earliest Christian documents (they pre-date the first of the gospels, which is Mark's). With the one exception of the resurrection, they mention *none* of Jesus' miracles. With Mark's Gospel we have accounts of the stilling of the waters, the raising of Jairus' daughter, the feeding of the multitude, the walking on water and various miracles of healing. Most of these miracles occur in Matthew and Luke, who used Mark as one of their sources. But in addition we now have not only the miraculous haul of fish and the healing of the high priest's servant's ear, but also the raising of the young man of Nain and the virgin birth. With John's Gospel, which was written some twenty years later, we find for the first time: the raising of Lazarus, the healing of the man born blind and the turning of water into wine. Though it would be unwise to draw any hard and fast conclusion from this comparison, it is, nevertheless, suggestive that the number of miracles associated with Jesus was increasing with time.

If earlier we experienced difficulty coming to terms with the realization that some of the material of the Old Testament was of mythical rather than historical origin, it is even more disturbing to find that elements of the New Testament similarly seem to lack historical authenticity. The seriousness of this discovery lies in the fact that, as we mentioned before, Christianity is essentially a historical religion – it depends upon certain New Testament events having actually taken place – and many Christians are of the opinion that once one starts questioning the historical truth of any part of the Bible, and particularly the New Testament, one has stepped on to a slippery slope. But this fear is, I believe, exaggerated. In tackling the authenticity of the miracle stories, one is looking at that part of the New Testament that is particularly vulnerable from the historical standpoint. In any case, like it or not, if the indications point in this direction, then we must in all honesty follow them and see where they lead.

Accepting that some of the miracle stories are not to be regarded as statements of historical fact, we must next ask how they came to be included in the biblical writings. What motive could the writers of the gospels have had? Are they attempts to deceive us, or what?

It is at this point, somewhat belatedly, that we come to grips with what in all likelihood is the true nature of many of the biblical miracle stories. At the start of our discussion, I pointed out that the early church was almost exclusively preoccupied with the interpretation of miracle stories and paid little heed to questions of historicity. We have gone to the very opposite extreme in our discussion, devoting all our energies to deciding whether the events actually happened. It is now time for us to redress the balance.

The clearest understanding of how miracle stories were used by New Testament writers is to be gained from a study of John's Gospel. We begin with an examination of the first of the miracles Jesus is said to have performed. It is a story which, we noted earlier, occurs only in John's Gospel: the turning of water into wine.

Our initial reaction to the account is likely to be one of scepticism. In the first place it can be argued that wine that runs out at a wedding feast is an embarrassment for the host to be sure, but hardly a matter to warrant the performance of a miracle. The guests were, in any case, so we are told, 'well drunk'. Jesus' mother, in pointing out the lack of wine, clearly expected him to do something about it. His reply, 'Woman, why turn to me? My hour has not come yet', is a statement that he is not to be dictated to, even by his closest relations; it also appears to be a flat rejection of the request – one which would be perfectly in accord with his earlier decision not to trivialize the use of his power. And yet we are led to believe that he relented later and agreed to go along with his mother's request. It seems out of character, even when it is acknowledged that the request did come from his mother, a person for whom he doubtless had a special regard. A further cause for concern is that stories of water being turned into wine were common among earlier religions; it was, for example, a feature of the cult of Dionysus, the Greek god of wine.

But we must be careful not to rush to too hasty a conclusion. For a start, we note that the story deals with a transformation involving wine. In the Christian context, transformations involving wine have a special significance; we are immediately put in mind of the transformation which is held to take place in the Communion Service – the one in which wine is changed, in some sense or other, into the Blood of Christ. John was writing at a time when the celebration of Holy Communion had already become well-established. We are therefore led to wonder whether John, in writing about water changing into wine, expected his readers to recognize that he was actually alluding obliquely to that other transformation. In both cases, a relatively common substance is elevated, through the power of God, into something more precious. The suspicion that this was indeed John's intention is strengthened by the observation that the word he uses to refer to the servants who bring the pots of water to Jesus is not the one he would normally have been expected to use; instead he uses the word for the deacons who assisted at the Holy Communion service. Next, we note that in response to Mary's request, Jesus does not respond by simply granting her wish: a little extra wine to cover an embarrassing deficiency. Instead, he creates the very best wine, as attested to by the steward of the feast, and an overflowing abundance of it – 120 to 180 gallons of it! This might be taken as illustrative of God's generous answer to prayer in which he grants us far more than we either desire or deserve. Next, we direct our attention to the original purpose of the water. We are told it had been intended for 'purification' (the washing of hands before the meal). This same water – whilst it had remained water – was incapable of meeting the needs of the feast. In the same way, adherence to the Jewish law had been inadequate to cleanse the Jewish people of sin; it required the coming of Jesus and his 'fulfilment of the law' before the people's needs could be met and their sins washed away. Was John expecting his readers to make this connection as well? Then we must not overlook the fact that the setting of the story is a marriage and that Jesus constantly referred to *himself* as a bridegroom. For example, when, on a later occasion, he was asked why his disciples did not fast, he was to say that whilst they had the bridegroom with them they could not mourn but eventually, when the hour came for the bridegroom to be taken away from them, then they would fast. Could it be that when Jesus at the wedding feast of Cana said 'My hour has not come yet', he did not mean that the time was not right for the performance of a miracle (which is the meaning we have so far attributed to it), but that the hour had not yet come for the bridegroom – meaning himself – to be taken away from his disciples? If this were the case, then he was saying, in effect, that the time was right for eating and drinking and so, rather than refusing to perform a miracle, he was in fact agreeing to it. Finally, we must not overlook the very opening words of the story: 'On the third day . . .' Though superficially John is saying that the wedding took place on the third day after the previous incident he had described, namely, a conversation with Nathanael, we cannot but wonder whether that was the real reason for beginning the narrative in that way. Almost certainly it was not. Knowing John, we suspect that he was drawing a deliberate parallel between the rejoicing of the wedding reception and that accompanying the resurrection of Jesus on that other third day.

If this is the first time you have come across this way of analysing a piece of biblical writing, I can well imagine your reactions at this point. It all seems rather far-fetched. One suspects that much too much is being read into what in truth is just a simple story that ought to be accepted or rejected at face value. Were this story to be uniquely open to this kind of analysis, then one would be right to view this approach with mistrust. But it is not. Confirmation that we are on the right track comes when we study other miracle stories of John. Here, we do not need to go digging below the surface to uncover allusions to a wider context – John himself explicitly points out the metaphors.

After feeding the multitude, for instance, Jesus has this to say: 'Do not work for food that cannot last, but work for food that endures to eternal life, the kind of food the Son of Man is offering you.' He goes on: 'I am the bread of life.' In John's treatment, the miracle story in which Jesus provides an endless supply of food becomes symbolic; it is illustrative of Jesus' ability to satisfy spiritual hunger and to offer life eternal.

After the miracle in which he cures the man born blind, Jesus enters into a discussion with the Pharisees about blindness – not physical blindness, but their own blindness to sin: 'It is for judgement that I have come into this world, so that those without sight may see and those with sight turn blind.' A little earlier he had spoken of himself as 'the light of the world'. Once again a physical miracle reinforces a spiritual message.

Before the raising from the dead of Lazarus, Jesus declares: 'I am the resurrection. If anyone believes in me, even though he dies he will live, and whosoever lives and believes in me will never die.' So we find the pattern repeated once more. A miraculous event serves to bring home yet another spiritual truth: eternal life is not something we have to wait for – it begins here and now in the midst of our earthly existence.

From these examples it is clear that, regardless of whether we are supposed to believe in the miracles as historical events, the prime purpose of these stories is that they convey inner spiritual meanings. Each story has something to teach us about the nature of Jesus and what he expects of us. The fact that John wrote mainly with Gentile readers in mind probably accounts for why he went to such pains to make these inner meanings explicit – he could not rely on his readers being familiar with Jewish ways of thought and styles of writing.

But what of the other gospels? Do they also contain miracle stories more concerned with spiritual truth than historical fact? The miraculous haul of fishes must surely belong to this category; it graphically illustrates with a physical analogy the words that accompanied that miracle: 'I will make you into fishers of men.' Likewise the healing of the high priest's servant's ear is an apt gloss on Jesus' injunction to his followers to put up the sword.

What of the virgin birth – the story of how Jesus came to be conceived of the Holy Spirit rather than by a man? Are we to understand this in the same manner? Certainly there are difficulties in accepting it as a straight account of an actual occurrence. In the first place, the story appears in only two of the gospels, those of Matthew and Luke. The other gospel writers ignore it. Indeed, there is no subsequent reference to it anywhere in the Bible. Even Paul in his deep theological arguments is silent about it. It is hard to resist the conclusion that, at the time the New Testament documents were being written, few people had heard of the story, or having heard of it, did not believe it even in those times. According to some scholars, the story has arisen from a misunderstanding. Matthew, in support of his story, quotes a well-known prophecy of Isaiah concerning the birth of the Messiah: 'A virgin will conceive and give birth to a son and they will call him Immanuel.' ('Immanuel' means 'God is with us'.) In so doing, he quoted from the Greek translation of the original Hebrew. Unfortunately for Matthew, the translation was incorrect; the original Hebrew referred simply to a 'young girl' – it did not use the word for 'virgin'. This error, so it is claimed, could have been the source of the story. Other authorities point to the prevalence of ancient stories in which gods visited the earth to have children by human mothers; they conclude that one of these stories could somehow have become attached to the Christian tradition.

Whichever of these theories is correct (if indeed either of them are), there can be no doubt about the underlying spiritual meaning of the story and the way Matthew and Luke make use of it. Basically the virgin birth story sets forth, in a particularly clear and direct manner, the Christian understanding of the nature of Jesus. This holds that Jesus was both God and man. He was not God dressed up to look like a man and only pretending to suffer; neither was he a mere man who went about pretending to be God. In Jesus we have the fusion of true God and true man. As man, he existed in time and space and was subject to all the restrictions and human needs we ourselves experience; as God, he existed outside time and space and possessed unlimited power. Important though this topic is, it is one I do not wish to pursue for the moment; this is better done later when I am able to set it in context with equally remarkable paradoxes that have come to light in modern science. Suffice to say for now, Christians believe that in some quite out-of-the-ordinary sense, beyond our full comprehension, Jesus was an amalgam of the human and divine. So, what better way to convey this difficult concept than through the idea that Jesus came into the world through the fusion of the Holy Spirit of God and a human virgin. Belief that Jesus is the Son of God is in no way dependent on the historical truth of the miracle; as we have seen, apart from Matthew and Luke, no other New Testament writer has needed to call upon it to back up the claim. But once granted that Jesus is the Son of God, there is no doubt that the virgin birth story conveys the essence of this truth with matchless skill.

By now you have probably gained the impression that I regard all miracle stories as no more than allegories and that it is wholly unimportant whether the miracles actually happened or not, provided one gives proper consideration to the underlying meanings. If so, let me conclude by saying why I believe certain miracles did in fact happen – why, under certain circumstances, I consider Jesus would have had no alternative but to perform one. I refer to the miracles of healing – not to those that have a psychosomatic explanation (or the special case of the healing of the servant's ear) but to the many other healing miracles that admit of no easy explanation – the instantaneous cure of leprosy, for example.

As a preliminary, we need to remind ourselves of the essence of the relationship between God and man. According to Christian belief, it is a relationship rooted in *love*. God loves us and we respond to him. Though we might repeatedly let him down and fall short of his standards, God's love for us remains at all times perfect. It was in order to demonstrate that love that he sent his Son to us.

So, with this in mind, let us imagine Jesus confronted by someone who is suffering. What is he to do? We know what we ourselves would do if faced with a loved one in distress; we would do all in our power to help. Jesus, as the perfect embodiment of God's love and concern for mankind, could hardly do less: he too must do all in his power to help. But what was the extent of his power? If he truly was the Son of God, the God who created the world and laid down the laws governing its working, would he not also possess the power to suspend those laws if he so desired? Surely he would and, possessing such power, he would be bound to use it on occasions such as these.

But does this not raise a difficulty? Would not this supernatural act, whilst effecting the cure, also tend to coerce the person concerned into believing in him and, therefore, offend against his earlier decision not to influence people in this way? No. A careful study of the acts of healing shows that in almost all cases the person cured is recorded as having already declared his or her faith in Jesus; failing that, their faith is implicit in their having come to Jesus to be healed. We may conclude that it was, in all probability, an invariable rule that Jesus would cure only those whose trust had been placed in him prior to the performance of the miracle. His repeated instructions to those cured that they should go away and tell no-one of what had happened would also be in line with his wish to play down the significance of the miracle as a means of converting people. There was certainly no question of the healing miracles being displays of power for their own ends. I am, therefore, inclined to accept most of the healing miracles as genuine.

Such a conclusion invites an obvious retort – particularly from readers who would like to believe in the literal truth of many more miracle stories than I would care to defend; if Jesus performed miracles of healing out of a sense of love and concern, why should he not have been stirred by a similar motive in respect of miracles of other kinds? With regard to the feeding of the multitude, for example, we read that he had 'compassion on the multitude'. Similarly, in the case of the raising of Lazarus, Jesus is described as being in 'great distress' at the sight of the sister of Lazarus weeping. This is fair comment. There were strong loving motives in these instances too. So perhaps

Jesus did indeed perform these miracles as well. I suspect he did not, but that is only my opinion.

If I had to summarize my own attitude towards miracles, I suppose I would put it like this. For the various reasons we have gone into, there hangs over many of the miracle stories a question mark concerning their historical veracity. Two thousand years after the event, it is now too late to find a way of settling the issue once and for all in a manner that would satisfy everyone. I suggest we lay the problem on one side. Instead, rather as the early church did, we ought to concentrate on their underlying meanings. It is here the true and lasting value of the stories is to be found. As with the ancient myths and the parables of Jesus – which also had no need to be rooted in real events – they possess deep inner truths. To the extent that the miracle stories continue to throw light on the nature of God and his relationship to man, so they will continue to command our respect and affection.

One final point: at no time have I called into question that God *could* have performed all the miracles had he so wished. Too often, discussions about miracles are clouded by the misunderstanding that when someone says that certain miracles probably did not happen, then this must be because he believes God incapable of performing them. That is not the case with me. In my view, the God who created the world and who laid down the laws governing its operation certainly possessed the power to suspend those laws if he so willed. The question is not whether he *could* have done it, but whether he actually *did* do it. As such, it becomes a straight matter of historical investigation. And when that investigation has to be based upon documents that, unlike our modern historical records, are theologically motivated – 'recorded so that you may believe that Jesus is the Christ, the Son of God' as John expressly puts it – there can be no easy answers.

9 The Touchstone of Christian Belief

There was one notable omission from our discussion of miracles: I said nothing about the resurrection of Jesus. This was quite deliberate. The resurrection is a miracle that stands in a class by itself. Christianity is built upon this event; remove it and the basis of all Christian belief is destroyed. Though we can, without much loss, suspend judgment over the historical truth of the other miracles, over this one there can be no hedging, no compromise. It is the climax of all four gospels. The very word 'gospel' itself, meaning good-news, refers specifically to the assertion that Jesus has risen from the dead; the gospel message is not, as some would think, that Jesus was a good man who gave sound advice in his Sermon on the Mount and set an example such that it would be nice were everyone to follow it. And not only is the resurrection integral to the gospels, it is the bedrock upon which all the other New Testament books are based; in any other setting they do not make sense.

It is not difficult to see how the resurrection acquires its distinctive position among the miracles: Christianity is more than a code of good conduct, more than an abstract philosophy; it is a loving relationship with a Jesus who is alive here and now. Without the resurrection, there could be no such relationship. Not only that, Jesus' resurrection holds out the promise that one day we, too, shall share in it and accordingly should be living our present life in that knowledge. The Easter story is clearly one we must examine with particular care.

We begin by asking whether the descriptions given have an authentic ring about them; do they *sound* like reports of something that has actually been seen to occur? It is well-known that genuine eyewitness accounts have certain features that set them apart from

65

fabricated stories – ingredients familiar to policemen having to investigate alibis and road accidents, or for that matter, to school teachers sorting out the circumstances leading up to a playground fight.

In the first place, it is unlikely that the account will follow a carefully structured logical sequence of the main points one needs to know. Instead, one is given a kaleidoscope of impressions with trivial, irrelevant details mixed up with the important ones; at times one wonders whether the witness will ever get to the point!

Secondly, one notes that moments of surprise and shock figure prominently in the account as though they are indelibly printed on the memory. Often the description of such unexpected occurrences is prefaced by a phrase like: 'To my dying day, I'll never forget the moment when . . .'

Thirdly, there are aspects the witness finds difficult to explain; sometimes these might even be aspects of their own behaviour which leave them looking rather foolish: 'I don't know what came over me; I must have been thinking of something else at the time . . .'

Finally, if several witnesses are involved, one expects not only broad agreement over the main points, but invariably a few minor contradictions and inconsistencies. Difficult though it sometimes is to understand how such discrepancies can arise, they are, nevertheless, one of the truly characteristic hall-marks of authentic, though imperfect, eyewitness accounts. It is when the suspects at the police-station, or the school-children in the headmaster's office, trot out exactly identical stories that one suspects collusion.

So we ask: are these indications of authenticity to be found in the gospel accounts of Easter?

For a start, let us look at the description of the two disciples going to the tomb. They set out together but one outruns the other to reach the tomb first. For some unstated reason, he does not go in immediately. Instead, he waits for his companion to arrive and then allows him to enter ahead of him. None of this, of course, is particularly important and one is left wondering why the writer bothered recording such inconsequential details. No reason, other than that was actually the way it happened and it was something that just stuck in the mind. The episode as described is a good example of the impressionistic nature of eyewitness accounts. It is followed by the moment of shock: they looked into the tomb – it was *empty*. They could hardly believe their eyes; the scene stamped itself on their memories, right down to the minute detail that the cloth originally over Jesus' face was lying a little apart from the other clothes. The key moment in the story and, as expected of a true account, one that is vividly recalled.

Turning to the story of the disciples walking along the road to Emmaus, we find an illustration of another of the features characteristic of eyewitness reports. Whilst they were walking, they were joined by Jesus who engaged them in conversation, but, extraordinary though it might seem, they did not recognize him. Even after they had invited him into the house and had sat down for a meal, they still did not know who he was. We can imagine their embarrassment when subsequently they had to recount the incident. How often they must have heard it said: 'But surely you must have known who he was! Do you mean to say you did not even recognize his voice?' It is a classic example of the way people can sometimes find themselves at a loss to explain their own behaviour. The account then goes on to give a further instance of what we have been calling a moment of shock. Jesus took the bread and broke it, a simple characteristic action, and 'their eyes were opened'. Why was this moment so special? I suspect that, although these two disciples had not been numbered among those present at the last supper, they had probably attended on similar occasions and, in any case, would have been told by the others of the strange prophetic words uttered by Jesus over the breaking of the bread the evening prior to his arrest: 'This is my body which will be given for you.' The recollection of those words, together with the sight of the bread being broken in exactly the manner they associated with Jesus, would have transformed an otherwise trivial incident into a moment of significance for those disciples at Emmaus.

We find the same ingredients in the story of Mary Magdalene's meeting with Jesus in the garden outside the tomb. She too was at first unable to recognize him; in her confusion she mistook him for the gardener. Then, for her too, there was to come the moment of shocked recognition, with a different sign this time: Jesus spoke her name. Why? What was so distinctive about Mary hearing her name spoken? I can only guess, but I imagine its significance lay in something that had happened between Mary and Jesus in the past. As is well known, she had been a prostitute prior to becoming one of his followers. Men had used her; to them she had been a body, not a person in her own right. But then Jesus had come on the scene and at some point would have called her by her name. In so doing, he would have given her what she had until that moment lacked: self-respect. She would not have forgotten the way he had said her name on that occasion and Jesus knew that as he stood before her in the garden.

How about the inconsistencies one expects genuine eyewitness accounts to have? Yes, there are some of those too. Matthew and Mark, for example, would have us believe that Jesus' appearances after his resurrection were confined to Galilee; Luke states them as occurring in or around Jerusalem; John has them occurring in both places. It would not have been all that difficult for the gospel writers to have checked out these details and got the facts right. One presumes they neglected to do so because they were more concerned in recording who the witnesses were and the circumstances surrounding the appearances rather than where they actually took place.

Though such slip-ups are forgiveable, indeed inevitable, the discrepancies must not amount to contradiction on matters of substance; recall I said that when several eyewitnesses are involved, there should be broad agreement on at least the main features of their stories. But there is one important aspect of the various accounts of Easter that appears at first sight worryingly inconsistent: the nature of Christ's risen body. Clearly, if a claim is made that someone has risen from the dead, the most obvious question to come to mind is: 'What kind of body is he supposed to have? Is it insubstantial, ethereal (leaving one to guess that the appearances might have been visions or hallucinations on the part of the so-called witnesses), or does it have similarities with a normal body in that it can exert forces and be touched?'

In the main, the accounts of Christ's resurrection describe his body as being the latter; he breaks bread, he eats food set before him, Thomas is invited to put his fingers into the nail holes in Jesus' hands and into the wound in his side. But one incident does not seem to fit in with this pattern; the occasion of Jesus' appearance to Mary

Magdalene in the garden. Here, he is said to have told her 'Touch me not; for I am not yet ascended unto the Father.' Curious. Why should he tell her not to touch, whereas he was to tell Thomas the opposite?

In point of fact, there is no problem. In the Greek version of the story, Jesus' statement to Mary can be translated either as 'Do not attempt to touch me', which is the meaning customarily placed on it and implies prohibition, or alternatively as 'Stop touching me', implying that Mary was already touching him, perhaps clinging to him. This latter meaning would be in line with the other descriptions of Christ's risen body. When, in addition, we reflect on the possible significance attached, to the phrase 'for I am not yet ascended to my Father', we find further reason for preferring the second translation. Whereas the first translation would seem to indicate that touching is permitted in heaven but not allowed here, a rather odd state of affairs, the second can be understood to mean that, although there will be plenty of opportunities in heaven for loving embraces, now is not the time because he has an urgent errand for her. She is to hurry to the disciples and let them know what has happened. There seems no doubt that the second translation is the one that conveys the original intention and it is this sense which all up-to-date translations of the Bible give to it.

Summing up so far then, we see that the descriptions given of the Easter events pass the first test: they show all the hallmarks of genuine eyewitness accounts. But, is this to say that the accounts of the resurrection are totally untouched by the tendency we noted in the previous chapter for stories to become elaborated and more fantastical with time?

No. The process is at work here as elsewhere. Mark's account of the discovery of the empty tomb mentions the presence of 'a young man in a white robe'. Later, in Matthew's Gospel, he is identified as an angel (this interpretation perhaps being helped by the fact that, in the first century, angels were not thought of as having wings). By the time we reach the gospels of Luke and John, we find the first angel joined by a second! Clearly what we are dealing with is not a pure, unsullied historical record.

But one must not conclude from this that the resurrection is just one more instance of a miracle story illustrating a divine truth through the description of an imagined physical occurrence. The strongest evidence against such a deduction is to be found not so much in what the resurrection accounts say, as in what they do *not* say. Consider: if the intention of the gospel writers had been to create a story that provided a visual image of the spiritual truth of Christ's victory over death, would they not have described the moment of victory itself? Jesus' emergence from the tomb would have been the very heart of the story. Thunder and lightning, the stone over the mouth of the tomb being flung to one side, Jesus' coming out resplendent, a voice from heaven announcing the significance of the moment, a heavenly choir sings his triumphant praises, on-lookers throw themselves to the ground in wonder and awe, etc., etc. But none of this appears in the gospels. As far as the actual moment of resurrection is concerned, they are silent. Or at least, almost silent. At one point in Matthew's Gospel there is a hint (but only a hint) that he was tempted to fill in some missing details! Unlike the other gospels which report the stone as having already been rolled aside before the women arrive and the angel(s) just sitting there, Matthew describes the angel in the act of descending from heaven and rolling the stone aside in the presence of the women – and to the accompaniment of a violent earthquake. But there his imagination stops.

Not so, the writer of the apocryphal 'Gospel of Peter'. As was his custom, he let his imagination rip. Starting from Matthew's modest addition, he develops the story into a full-blown account of the moment of resurrection. Two men, encircled by a great light, descend and roll the stone away. The on-lookers 'see three men coming out of the tomb, the two supporting the one, and a cross following them, and the heads of two reached as far as heaven, but that of Him that was led overtopped the heavens. And they heard a voice from heaven saying, Hast thou preached to them that sleep? And a response was heard from the cross, Yea.' And so the story goes on. It is an account fully in the tradition of miracle story writing. As such, it stands in stark contrast to the accounts of the resurrection to be found in the gospels.

The fact that the gospel accounts are so radically different from what we would expect of a conventional miracle story cannot be over-stressed. Jewish miracle stories were invariably written to a standard pattern. They were divided into three sections: (i) the scene is set in enough detail to make it clear that what was to follow had indeed to be miraculous (Lazarus' body already in a state of decay, or the man having been blind from birth, for example); (ii) the miracle itself is described with accompanying words and actions; and (iii) the consequences of the miracle are described (the lame man picks up his bed and walks, the on-lookers are astonished and so on). The resurrection accounts in the gospels do not conform to this pattern; they omit altogether the all-important middle section. There can only be one explanation of this: what we are dealing with here is not the usual kind of miracle story, but a set of reports from eyewitnesses. The fact that there is no report of the resurrection event itself is simply due to the fact that there was no one around to witness it.

So, granted that these are accounts which are meant to be taken at face-value, the next question is: 'Do we actually believe them? What are the alternatives? Are there any explanations not involving a resurrection?'

By way of answer, we first note that there existed at the time a group of people who would have been only too glad to seize any opportunity of discrediting the story if they could: the chief priests. Having got rid of someone whom they took to be a blasphemer and rabble-rouser, the last thing they wanted was for a story to go the rounds claiming 'proof' that they had in fact put to death the Son of God.

The quickest way to put a stop to the rumours would have been to go to the tomb, take out the body, and put it on display. The fact that this was not done can only mean the body was not there. So whether or not there was a resurrection, of one thing we can be certain: the tomb was empty. Any alternative to the resurrection must therefore involve some person or persons removing the body. There is no reason why the chief priests or their supporters would have taken it; as we have seen, all their efforts would have been directed towards finding it and showing it to the public. The finger of suspicion has to point to the disciples and to Jesus' other followers. And just as we would expect, this was the accusation put around by the priests at the time. But if it is unreasonable to think of the chief priests removing the body, is it any more likely that the disciples would have done it? Where was *their* motive? Immediately we can rule out any question of personal benefit; no one stood to gain anything other than ridicule and, in some cases, their own death. How about devotion to the cause – would not sheer fanaticism be sufficient motive? After all, when the leader of a popular movement has been unjustly put to death, it is only natural for his followers to be outraged and seek retribution, even at terrible cost to themselves. This will not do, either. The disciples did not seek revenge; those who went to their deaths were not impelled by feelings of anger but rather of joy. In any case, the most powerful, emotive, rallying point the disciples had was the *dead* Jesus, not the living one. Many a cause has thrived on the death of a leader who proved himself more potent dead than alive. By stealing and hiding the body and making up a silly story that Jesus was not really dead, the disciples would have recklessly thrown away the capital they could otherwise have made out of Jesus' martyrdom. We must not kid ourselves into thinking that the resurrection story would have sounded more plausible in those days than it does in our own time. It would have attracted just as much scepticism and derision then as it does now. The whole episode as described simply does not make sense.

As for the idea that the disciples made up the story of the resurrection as one last attempt to convince the Jewish people that Jesus was the Messiah after all, this really does not stand up to scrutiny either. Whilst it was true that the gospel writers lost no chance in pointing out how the events of Jesus' life repeatedly fulfilled the prophecies of old concerning the coming of the Messiah, there was *no* Old Testament prophecy that the Messiah would rise from the dead. The resurrection came as a complete surprise. So their belief that Jesus was the Messiah provided no incentive to the disciples to invent the story.

Quite apart from the lack of motive, there is another difficulty: if the body was stolen, then the theft and subsequent cover-up must have been effected by what can only rank as the most remarkable conspiracy of all times. It was not as though it was the work of just a couple of fanatics who might, without too much difficulty, have managed to keep the truth to themselves. There were many people who claimed to have seen the risen Jesus: the disciples, the women and on one occasion a crowd of five hundred. Is it remotely conceivable that such a heterogeneous collection of people could have been welded into a conspiracy of this nature? Among Jesus' close followers, would there not have been at least one or two who would have refused to join in the fraudulent claims? Or, having all agreed to perpetrate the deception, are we to believe that under the enormous pressures brought to bear on the early church not a single one of them broke the silence? After all, it is not as though they were hardened criminals and habitual liars, experienced in such ways. On the contrary, they were followers of someone noted for his sincerity, truth and inherent goodness. It would have required a remarkable reversal of character for those living in the closest communion with Christ and under the influence of his teaching suddenly to renege on their ideals and practice wholesale deception.

Mind you, an astonishing change *did* come over Jesus' followers a short while after his death, but it was a transformation of a different kind. At the time of the crucifixion and in the days immediately following, the disciples were disorganized and frightened. They hid in locked rooms, scared that even though they had now deserted their leader, they might still be sought out by the Jewish authorities and made to suffer a similar fate. Suddenly, all this changed. The defeatism and cowardice disappeared. Overnight they became courageous, willing to die and almost euphoric with the sense of a great victory having been accomplished. Had this radical change of attitude been confined to Jesus' immediate circle of friends, one could perhaps pass it off as collective hysteria. But it was not. Others from outside Jesus' immediate band of followers became caught-up in the new spirit. Remarkable among these was Christ's own brother, James. Neither James nor any of the other brothers appear to have had any understanding of, or sympathy for, what Jesus was doing during his ministry. It was this indifference that had led Jesus to say: 'A prophet is only despised in his own country, among his own relations and in his own house.' There was also the incident when Jesus' mother and the brothers came to take him home because they were 'convinced he was out of his mind'. But following Jesus' death and presumed resurrection, James was converted. He was to become the respected and much-loved head of the Christian movement in Jerusalem. As recorded by

Josephus (an independent historian who was unsympathetic to Christianity), James was eventually stoned to death for the cause in AD 62.

Noteworthy though the transformation wrought in James was, it by no means ranks as the most famous post-resurrection conversion; that distinction belongs to Saul of Tarsus, later to become St Paul. Who could possibly have foreseen that Christianity's arch-enemy would have been won over? What, other than a most extraordinary occurrence, could have caused him of all people to undergo a change of heart?

These changes in the way people behaved date from a time soon after the crucifixion. There can be no doubt something very special must have happened then, something capable of making the most unlikely people willing to sacrifice their lives with seemingly reckless abandon for a cause they had once thought lost, or to which they had previously been indifferent or hostile. Nor were these changes passing phases or temporary derangements of the mind; those affected were to remain so permanently. Christians believe an adequate explanation of all this can only be found in the resurrection.

Finally, no discussion of the resurrection would be complete without looking at what Jesus, during his life-time, had said about the resurrection that was to come and about the after-life in general. On several occasions, he alluded to the fact that he would rise again from the dead, though at the time few, if any, had any idea of what he meant. Thoughts of eternal life were, in fact, never far from him. It was a promise he held out to his followers: 'There are many rooms in my Father's house; if there were not, I should have told you. I am going now to prepare a place for you.' Statements such as these put us on the spot. They are unambiguous and uncompromising. We must make up our minds as to whether we think they are true or not. If they are not, then Jesus told lies – his whole life was a lie and he encouraged people to sacrifice their lives for a promise of eternal life which he knew had no substance. Could a man, who in all other respects was the embodiment of goodness and sincerity, practise such cruel deception? Perhaps he was mad. But surely not; the world has never known a man whose teaching was so infused with sanity, wisdom and penetrating insight.

74

So how do we summarize this discussion? We have looked at accounts of the resurrection and found that they appear to be eye-witness descriptions of something that really happened. The subsequent behaviour of all those involved was fully consistent with what they said had happened. We looked for alternatives to the resurrection story; none seemed plausible. There is no motive for why the disciples should have stolen the body. It is barely credible that a conspiracy of such proportions could have remained intact. Furthermore, from what was known of the character of the people involved in the affair, they were not the sort to get involved in such deception. Even Jesus himself would stand implicated. Finally, we have noted the remarkable changes wrought in the lives, not only of his followers, but of others who had previously been unsympathetic or antagonistic.

The resurrection accounts are therefore everything one could reasonably expect a true description of an actual happening to be. That being the case, why is it that so many people, nevertheless, remain unconvinced in the face of the evidence?

No one who has ever looked at a corpse and touched the cold, stiff form can find it easy to believe that the life that once animated that body is now anything but irrevocably finished. Call it an irrational impulse if you like, but it is there and has to be answered. This feeling is the one and only thing that stands in the way of acceptance of the resurrection story. It is so strongly felt that no mere written account of any resurrection could hope to satisfy it.

Suppose, for a moment, you had yourself come face to face with an example of a resurrection; someone who everyone knew to have died comes and visits you, talks with you and touches you. How would you set about convincing others that this had happened? Are there any words that would be likely to convince them? Even if your whole life were demonstrably, indeed startlingly, changed by the encounter, would that compel others to believe your story? No. Though every detail of your account and behaviour was consistent with such a meeting and though there was no other adequate explanation, you would still find it impossible to convince the majority that you were speaking the truth. The gut feeling of the inevitability and finality of death would in the end defeat you.

This being so, you should not be surprised at your own scepticism concerning the gospel accounts of the resurrection of Jesus. You cannot expect any written account of such an event to be wholly convincing; none would be capable of completely overcoming the innate, built-in prejudice that death marks the end. And this remains so even when one admits to oneself that that is all it is – a prejudice.

Were we to be weighing up the evidence in a Scottish law court, we would have an easy way out of our dilemma: we would duck the issue and return a verdict of 'not proven'. But this is not an option open to us. Either we lead our lives as though Jesus were alive with us, or as though he were not. Non-acceptance of the Easter story inevitably implies acceptance of the alternative – the body-stealing alternative which, as we have seen, has all the evidence, such that it is, stacked against it and nothing to commend it, other than it allows us to retain our prejudice in the finality of death. There can be no half-way measures. After all, Jesus himself said, 'He who is not with me is against me'. So whilst we delay making up our minds on the issue, we are, by default, identified with the alternative to the resurrection. But is that *consciously* the view we wish to support?

Before deciding to throw in our lot with one side or the other, there is, fortunately, one further piece of evidence to consider; in the end it is the one piece of evidence that counts. It arises from the simple recognition of the fact that if the resurrection story is correct, then Jesus is alive – now. This in turn means that it should be possible to contact him directly and so receive first-hand evidence.

For this possibility to be realized, action is required on our part; we need to do an experiment. What that experiment is I shall shortly describe. But, before doing so, I want to point out that from here on our investigation into the question of the resurrection will parallel the type of investigation carried out in science. I said in my introduction that there was a remarkable similarity between the methods used in matters of belief and those used in science. The next chapter draws this parallel and sets the stage for the experiment which ultimately provides the proof we have been seeking – the proof of the resurrection.

10 Scientists at Work

How does a scientist go about his work of searching out the secrets of nature? To give you some feel for what it can be like, let me recount a story drawn from my own experience.

A few years ago, theoretical physicists began talking about the possibility of there being a new property of matter. (I should perhaps explain that physicists tend to divide into two types: experimentalists like myself, responsible for setting up and performing experiments, and theoreticians who try to interpret the observations, often with the help of mathematics.) Through studying their equations, the theoreticians noted that they would look simpler and more manageable if it could be assumed that this new property existed.

Matter, as we know it, is characterized by various properties. Some are familiar to us in ordinary everyday life: for example, mass – the property that determines that one object is heavier than another; and electric charge – responsible for the working of electrical appliances in the home and the way garments sometimes cling when taken off or removed from a tumble drier. In addition to these familiar properties, there are others that reveal their presence only under certain special laboratory conditions. The newly predicted property was one of these rarer kinds.

The prediction was based on the feeling that the equations *ought* to be more symmetrical, more beautiful. If you are one who has always regarded mathematics with distaste, it might seem to you unlikely that scientists could think of equations as being beautiful; nevertheless, physicists are guided quite often by what can only be described as an aesthetic sense and this was one such occasion.

At first, the suggestion was greeted with scepticism; none of the investigations carried out to that date had shown any behaviour that could not be perfectly well explained in terms of the already established properties. But after a while, one or two reports did start coming in of observations that appeared a little odd. The theoreticians got excited; they claimed their proposal could explain the anomolous behaviour, albeit in a rather roundabout way. They became so enamoured of this hypothetical property that they gave it a name, a rather silly one; they called it 'charm'.

Further speculation led to a suggestion as to why charm might, until that time, have eluded direct detection. Its existence was exceedingly fleeting; no sooner was a charm-carrying particle produced than it broke up, the charm property being lost in the process. Tentative calculations showed that such particles would be around for only one ten-million-millionth of a second. Though we experimentalists had been used to handling fairly short-lived particles, we had certainly not anticipated dealing with anything quite as quick as *that*! Had such particles been produced in our previous experiments, we would indeed have overlooked them.

And yet the detection of such particles was not impossible. A unique combination of different types of equipment, specially assembled for this one purpose, could conceivably overcome the difficulties. 'So,' one might think, 'what's the problem? Go ahead, do the experiment and see whether charm exists.' But things are not that simple. Every experiment exacts its price in terms of manpower, time and money. This particular experiment would be a major undertaking: thirty highly qualified physicists and an army of technicians and engineers working for two years to plan and execute the project, at a cost of £1,000,000! At the time (the mid 1970s), I was laying odds of five to one against charm existing, so was not all that keen on doing the experiment. Only the theoreticians were offering shorter odds, but they were prejudiced and, in any case, they would not be the ones running the risk of wasting their time and effort, and the taxpayers' money, looking for something that was not there.

To cut a long story short, after much heart-searching and despite many reservations, I and some colleagues from other universities eventually did join forces and mount the experiment; it was clearly the only way to settle the issue. Eighteen months later, to our surprise and delight (to say nothing of my discomfiture as an amateur book-maker), the first direct sighting of a particle carrying charm was made. It behaved almost exactly as the theoreticians had predicted. The first example found in my own laboratory was greeted with yells of excitement. People came running down the corridor from nearby offices to see what all the commotion was about. They found me hugging and dancing with my technicians (who, I would add, are attractive young ladies); the champagne bottles, brought in on the off-chance that they might conceivably be needed one day, were duly opened. Telegrams announcing the news were despatched to friends throughout Europe and back came a flood of congratulations.

None of this joy and excitement appears in the final scientific paper. Neither does it contain any hint of the doubts that had originally marked the launching of the experiment, nor the frustrations, disappointments, arguments and disagreements, the effort and sheer tedium that sometimes characterized its execution. That paper, to be found within the covers of a learned journal, is the calm, rationalized account of the bare facts; it is the permanent record of those observations that other scientists need to know in order to build their own theories and mount their own experiments. It is the way we scientists present our results: cold, systematic and logical. I suppose it is this dehumanized manner in which we always seem to package our discoveries that makes it so difficult for those outside science to discover what being a scientist is really like.

There are a number of points to note about the way charm was discovered. Firstly, in the performance of the experiment, there were no half-measures. The fact that I was laying odds of five to one against a positive result did not mean that I felt we should be putting in correspondingly less effort. Once one has decided to look for charm, then, regardless of any preconceptions as to the likely outcome, one has to go in with both feet and invest a one hundred per cent effort. If there is to be any chance at all of finding it, one has to do everything that would be necessary to obtain a positive result, should it later transpire that a positive result is the right one.

Secondly, if charm had not existed, we would not at the end of the experiment have persuaded ourselves that it did, simply in order to justify all the effort we had put in. There have been many other experiments I could have described where scientists, myself included, have searched just as diligently for something, but have drawn a blank. When this happens, one just accepts the disappointment and the thought of having perhaps wasted a portion of one's working life and hopes for better luck next time.

Lastly, the experiment was something of an act of faith. We experimentalists did not suddenly and irrationally decide, as on a wild impulse, to go ahead with that experiment; there was motivation behind it. The experiment was undertaken only after we had carefully weighed up the arguments produced by the theoreticians. This line of reasoning did not prove the existence of charm and so a positive result to the experiment could not be assured. What the arguments did show was that it was sensible and respectable to go ahead and look for charm and that the act of looking was the only way to resolve the matter. The line of reasoning justified the performance of the experiment; it was the experiment, and that alone, which justified belief in charm. Acts of faith such as this – that is to say, actions taken specifically to test the truth of a seemingly reasonable but as yet unproven claim – are an indispensible feature of scientific enquiry. Almost every experiment undertaken is such an act – a leap into the unknown but, as we have seen, not one that needs to be irrational.

11 Taking on Trust

It is an act of faith that provides proof of the resurrection claim. In many ways, we shall find it to be similar to that which brought proof of the existence of charm. Not that acts of faith are confined to the heady spheres of religion and science. We find the same kind of thing happening in almost every walk of life. Time and again one can get just so far by reasoned argument, but then no further. In order to reach one's goal, some sort of action is required. The line of argument stops short, with its direction at the end-point indicating where final proof might lie, but it does not itself take one there. It is the leap of faith that spans the gap.

There are many examples I could quote. Take for instance, the way I allow other people to service my car. I am ashamed to admit that, even though I am a physicist, I know virtually nothing about cars; I have to rely on the local garage. When I put the car in for a service, I do so in the hope that the mechanics will do their job properly and that I will not subsequently find myself wrapped round a lamp-post as a result of faulty brakes. When I come to collect the car, I do not know for certain that my confidence in the mechanics is justified; that assurance can only come later from the act of driving the car out of the forecourt and finding that I subsequently arrive home safely.

Or perhaps I am dining out. How am I to know in advance that the food in a particular restaurant will be prepared hygienically? I could inspect the kitchen, I suppose, but I would not have the nerve to ask. No, the proof of the pudding is in the eating – in this case literally so!

Posting parcels at Christmas can be a risky business. One must hand them in on the unproven assumption that those responsible for collecting, sorting, transporting and delivering them, will neither lose, damage nor steal them. Once again the only way of finding out whether the assumption is justified is to give it a try.

When a new aircraft has been produced, it does not matter how skilful the designers, how expert the engineers and mechanics, or how thorough the inspection procedures and quality control, one cannot have full confidence in its safety and performance until it is test-flown.

Not for nothing is marriage described as 'taking the plunge', a leap into the unknown. No matter how long the period of getting to know each other, or how well the interests and temperaments appear to be matched, there remains an element of risk; there is no crystal ball in which to see how the two personalities will later develop and whether these changes will make the couple grow apart or draw them together closer still. It is only in retrospect that one can judge the success of a marriage.

Obviously one could go on giving further examples. This is especially so in a technological society where we have all come to depend on each other to a much greater extent than previously. Before industrialization, one more-or-less had to fend for oneself and for one's own family. Nowadays, few, if any, can claim to live self-sufficient lives; instead we have come to rely on the specialisms of others. Because it is impracticable always to be checking up on what others do for us, we are forced to exercise trust. Without it our modern society could not function.

These various acts of faith have features in common. For instance, in none of the examples given need the act be capricious or irresponsible. Before committing oneself to the course of action, there is scope for exercising commonsense. Prior to visiting the restaurant, for instance, there are elementary precautions one can take: avoiding grubby back-street cafes; making sure it at least looks clean and decent; and perhaps acting on the recommendation of a friend. In any case, it can be argued that it is in the interests of the restaurant owner and the employees to avoid a food-poisoning scandal and so they are probably in the habit of taking care. So, although there is no certainty, reasoning, as far as it goes, would have one believe that the risk is an acceptable one. The same can be true of any of the other examples mentioned. Though each step must, by its nature, be something of a leap in the dark, it can be a sensible one; it can be thought of as an extension to commonsense in that it effectively takes an investigation further than would otherwise be possible. The proof sought is to be found by looking back from the vantage point gained by the leap of faith.

In none of the examples was the person involved being gullible. Admittedly each act was based on some implied assumption: that the food in the restaurant would not cause ill effects; that the posted parcels would arrive; and that the aircraft was airworthy. That does not mean that the person committing the act had convinced himself from the outset that the assumption was necessarily correct; he presumably had grounds for believing that it might be, but he did not know for sure. Indeed, in the case of the new aircraft design, the whole purpose of the test-flight is to find out whether the assumption of airworthiness is true or not. Acts of faith, therefore, are not so much a matter of what one *believes*, as of what one *does* in order to learn more.

In each case the commitment to the act was one hundred per cent. One either drives the car out of the garage forecourt, or one does not; one either posts the parcel, or one does not. But note that complete commitment to the act in no way prejudices one's judgment of the final outcome: if one ends up with food poisoning, or the aircraft crashes, or the parcels fail to arrive, there is no question of convincing oneself otherwise simply because the action was based on the assumption of a different result.

These various points, all of which applied with equal force to the search for charm, are now to be borne in mind as we turn, at last, to the act of faith that leads to proof of the resurrection.

12 An Experiment with Prayer

Recall that our study of the Easter story ended inconclusively. As far as reason alone was concerned, the evidence, such that it was, seemed to be pointing to the conclusion that Jesus might well have risen from the dead. There certainly appeared no plausible alternative. And yet, the gospel accounts did not provide clinching proof – certainly not of a kind that would compel belief. So where do we go from here?

It is my belief that one ought never to have looked to the gospel accounts to provide such proof. I see them instead as analogous to the lines of reasoning that led up to the various acts of faith we have been considering. The gospel writers were no more able to prove the truth of their assertions by argument alone, than were, say, the theoretical physicists in respect of the existence of charm. The most one should have expected from the gospels was an indication as to whether it was reasonable and sensible to embark on some course of action that would take the investigation further. I believe that case to have been made.

George Fox, the founder of the Society of Friends (the Quakers), once said: 'I came to know God experimentally.' That exactly sums up the approach we shall ourselves now adopt.

The act of faith to which the gospels point is *prayer*. It is through prayer that people of various religions, not only Christianity, come face-to-face with God. But for Christians there is an added dimension: prayer is also their means of getting to know Jesus at first hand. As they pray, they experience the presence of the risen Jesus – and this is for them the final proof of the resurrection.

On the face of it, praying is easy. Yet it is something that most people are reluctant to try out. To some extent this is understandable.

No self-respecting person wants to develop the habit of talking to himself and there is bound to be the suspicion at first that this is all there is to prayer. But this reluctance really does not make sense when one stops to consider. After all, one is perfectly prepared to engage in acts of faith in other walks of life, so why feel uniquely vulnerable to the charge of being gullible when it comes to prayer? If it is considered respectable to go looking for a property of matter that might not be there, why is it any different if one goes looking for a God who might also not be there? And if physicists are in little danger of convincing themselves that their experiments point to the existence of charm if in truth there is no such thing, why should anyone consider that one is more likely to talk oneself into a false belief in God? A person entering into the experiment of prayer ought, I feel, to have as much confidence in his own integrity as I do in mine when I embark upon a scientific experiment.

This is not really the place for me to go into a detailed description of how one should pray; there are many others better qualified than I to advise on that subject. Nevertheless, having introduced the topic and it being so central to our discussion, I feel I ought to say just a little about it, particularly to those who have had little or no previous experience of praying and are unlikely to go out and buy a book about it.

All you really need to know about the mechanics of prayer comes from the recognition of the obvious: prayer is a form of communication. As such, it has many points of similarity with our normal ways of communicating with people. In the first place, in order to develop a close relationship with another person, one needs to have regular contact and be prepared to devote time to it. You should not under-estimate how long it might take to establish meaningful contact with God. Some are lucky, or are unknowingly well-prepared and receptive, and break through almost immediately; others take longer. It is essential, therefore, to get into the habit of setting aside time on a regular basis – say five minutes a day. Even this modest beginning can be difficult to arrange when you live in a household with others, but, with determination and a little ingenuity, it can be done. (Try locking yourself in the toilet if all else fails!) You should also be prepared to stick to this routine of daily prayer for quite some time.

How long? Well, one yardstick might be the length of time we physicists spent looking for charm. My colleagues and I spent two years on a search that could well have been fruitless. That being so, I reckon it is not asking too much that you should be prepared to spend five minutes a day for a couple of years looking for a God who might not exist. Ultimately, it is more important for you to settle the issue of whether God exists or not, than it was for me to discover whether there really was such a thing as charm.

Prayer is not a matter of 'saying one's prayers'; that might be all right for small children but not for adults. There is much more to prayer than the parrot-like recitation of set-pieces, no matter how beautifully they might be phrased. I am not in any way decrying the excellent prayers to be found, for example, in the Book of Common Prayer; they are couched in fine language and have their place and use, particularly in public worship. But in private prayer it is more important that you should think for yourself; you should speak directly from the heart of those things that concern you most. Talk about yourself and about those closest to you. Discuss your hopes and aspirations, your fears, problems and disappointments. Be utterly frank with God – including the fact that you have doubts as to whether he is there – he is aware of your lack of conviction.

Communication needs to be two-way. Do not talk incessantly; pause frequently so that God can come through to you, even though his contribution is through silence. That might sound odd at first, but it is not so. Perhaps the deepest, most loving form of communication between two people can be through silence – an elderly married couple, for instance, spending an evening together, each quietly getting on with reading or knitting, but conscious of the other's presence. It can be that way too with God. Cultivate an awareness of the reality of silent communication.

Each session ought to be preceded by the reading of a few verses from the Bible. Use a modern translation, like the Jerusalem or Good News Bible – one that has the material conveniently divided up into self-contained sections, with headings, which make it easier to know where it would be appropriate to start and stop reading a passage. The purpose of such reading is to become immersed in the personality of God – to get on to his wavelength. For Christians, the clearest image of God is to be found in the person of Jesus, so they concentrate their readings on the accounts of his life and teachings. In this way, they come to understand what he stood for and how he thought about issues and this, in turn, helps them appreciate the nature of God's thoughts. In any deep human relationship, one needs to know as much as possible about the other person.

Approach your task sympathetically and with determination. Remember that in the search for charm the effort put in by the physicists bore no relation to their personal misgivings and doubts concerning the likely outcome – we went into the project wholeheartedly, prepared to do everything in exactly the manner required to find charm on the assumption that it actually did exist. So, too, must you be totally committed to your prayer, holding nothing back, quietly assured that if Jesus is not there, you will not deceive yourself into thinking he is.

And what of the likely outcome? What is the nature of the evidence you can expect prayer to provide as to the reality of God and of the living Jesus? One thing is pretty certain: there will be no physical manifestation of his presence – no voice from heaven, no ghostly apparition or vision, no blinding light. If this is the kind of proof you are seeking, you will be disappointed. The evidence that you have been in contact with God is not to be found in some external happening. Rather you must look for it in changes brought about in *yourself*.

This is not so very different from what takes place in ordinary communication between people. In day-to-day interactions with those about us, there are two aspects to be distinguished: the means and the ends. There are different means of communication: voice, telephone, letter, telegram, a recorded message on tape, a wink, a frown, a squeeze of the hand, a kick under a table. These are passing phenomena of little significance in themselves. What really matters is the message and the effect it is designed to produce on the other person; the same ends can be served by a variety of means.

Consider some of the ways you might be affected by contact with others. You might, for instance, have a problem. You have been wrestling with it for some time, but you keep going round in circles making no progress. What you need is the injection from outside of some new idea – one that will break the vicious circle and allow your thoughts to be channelled into a new direction. It is for this reason we take our troubles to other people; we discuss them with friends, relations, teachers, doctors, social workers, marriage guidance counsellors, solicitors and so on. Or perhaps it is not so much a specific problem that troubles you, but a general feeling of anxiety and tension; being with someone who is equable and calm can help allay fears. You might be depressed; seeking out someone who is always cheerful can help shake off the blues. You might have lost heart over something you have undertaken; a word of encouragement can bring back determination. Possibly you are complacent or insensitive in the way you have treated someone; criticism can stir you to make amends. Perhaps you are in love and find the mere presence of the other a source of happiness.

The common feature of these and all ways you come into contact with others is that you are *affected* by their presence. Long after they have left you, you can remain affected. It might be a change of thinking, mood, awareness, or motivation. These changes then evidence themselves through your adoption of courses of action you would not otherwise have taken.

For each of these examples of communication between people, it is possible to point to identically the same thing happening between a person and God in the act of prayer. For example, take the case where one has a problem. Time and again, I have found my own thoughts going round in circles until eventually I have taken the problem to him. Occasionally, the problem is solved with breathtaking directness; almost before I have explained to him what is on my mind, he seems to be saying 'And about time too – what kept you?' and the answer comes. Sometimes the solution is not so direct; instead, my thoughts are deflected into some new channel, as though he had said, 'Stop for a moment; have you thought of this . . . ?' Following up this fresh line of thought, I have found it eventually leading to the answer. These occasions I think of as being rather like encounters with marriage guidance counsellors or psychotherapists where, instead of being given a pat answer to the problem, one is encouraged to discover one's own solution. On yet other occasions, prayer causes the problem simply to go away; it is not that the problem is resolved

– it is just that one sees it in a different light and it no longer seems that important.

Tackling our problems is only part of what God does through the medium of prayer. He offers encouragement and reassurance, gives purpose and direction to life; he can quicken our conscience and make us more aware of the needs of others, he can challenge us to some course of action, open up the possibility of new interests and experiences; above all, he envelops us in love and leads us to the realization that we are wanted, we matter to him.

It is because changes such as these are continually being brought about through prayer that people come to accept that they are not just talking to themselves when they pray; they are encountering another person. Moreover, in time they come to appreciate that, surprisingly, all the changes made in them by these encounters turn out ultimately to be to their benefit. I say 'surprisingly' because much of the advice received and the lines of action one is encouraged to follow appear at first sight to lead in the opposite direction to where one would oneself have expected to find personal happiness and fulfil-ment. The guidance offered is based on ideas of loving one's enemies, turning the other cheek, giving away possessions and money, devoting time to the service of others instead of going all out to enjoy oneself, the practice of self-control and discipline and so on – courses of action that seem to have little to do with serving one's own interests.

But all this is exactly how Jesus said it was. The God whom one encounters in prayer is the very same God of whom Jesus spoke – the very same God Jesus revealed in the way he lived his own life. Indeed, for Christians it becomes increasingly difficult to disentangle in their minds whether they are praying to God the Father or to Jesus. Some-times it is like talking to the Father with Jesus at one's side, at other times it is like holding a conversation directly with Jesus. But of one thing there is no doubt: Jesus is there. On reaching this point, any question of whether Jesus' presence is real or not – any question as to whether the resurrection really happened – simply evaporates; there can be only one answer.

Many who embark on prayer do not reach this conclusion. The kind of evidence they want is not the kind offered. Whilst expecting some outward, visible manifestation of God's presence, they overlook the subtler changes wrought in their own behaviour and attitudes – changes that are the testimony they seek. Or, if they do admit to such changes, they regard such indirect evidence as suspect.

I have to agree that, at first sight, it does appear paradoxical that one must look to changes in one's own behaviour in order to find evidence for someone else's existence. But, strange to say, this is not as unusual as you might think. At its deepest layers of investigation, science, in its domain, offers evidence that is no more direct. Proof of the existence of the fundamental properties of matter – those concepts upon which all science is based – is just as intangible.

Take, for instance, electric charge. How do we know there is such a thing? No one has actually seen it, so it cannot be a case of 'seeing is believing'. In fact, all we ever observe of electric charge is the way it induces changes of behaviour in nearby objects. For example, the assumption that electric charge exists allows us to explain why nylon garments stick together on being withdrawn from a tumble-drier. We say the clothes have acquired an electric charge through the way they rubbed against each other whilst revolving in the drier and it is the force of attraction between these charges that causes the clothes to cling. But it is sticking clothes we see, not the electric charge. The existence of the charge is inferred from the behaviour of the clothes.

Once granted that there might be such a thing as electric charge, we can go on to explain other phenomena, for example a flash of lightning. Here we suppose there to be a stream of tiny particles, electrons, carrying the electric charge. Through the forces exerted by these charges on the surrounding atoms of air, energy is released in the form of a flash of light. A satisfactory explanation, but one that is now removed one further stage from direct observation. Not only have we not seen electric charge, we have not even seen the particles that are supposed to be carrying the charge (electrons being much too small to be seen in any microscope no matter how powerful). All that is actually seen is the flash of light. And yet scientists are agreed on the existence of electrically charged electrons because, once granted that assumption, they can go on to explain flashes of lightning and a host of other features of the physical world.

How about that familiar property: mass? How do we know, for

example, that the moon possesses a mass and that it is smaller than that of the earth? Such a conclusion can be drawn from an observation of the antics of astronauts jumping up and down on the moon's surface. The reason they do not go floating off into space is that they are attracted back by the gravitational mass of the moon. The reason they are able to jump higher on the moon than on earth is that the mass of the moon is not as great as that of the earth, so the force of attraction is smaller. At least, this is how we choose to explain the phenomenon. But note we are not actually observing the mass itself; all we see are cavorting astronauts. It is the behaviour brought about in the astronauts which leads us to attribute a mass to the moon.

I could give further examples, but those I have mentioned already serve to make the point; science postulates the existence of certain fundamental properties of matter in order to explain observed phenomena, but the observed phenomena are not the properties themselves – they are behavioural patterns induced by the properties. The fact that the behaviour we observe can be consistently and predictably accounted for in this way is the justification for believing in the existence of the properties.

This being so, I find it hard to understand why the evidence for Jesus' presence – that is to say, the evidence for the resurrection – should be considered in any way less firm than that for electric charge, mass, charm, etc. If I, as a scientist, am persuaded of the reality of these quantities because of their ability to explain a wide range of physical behaviour, why should I not, as a Christian, be equally convinced of the reality of the resurrection by its ability to explain all that happened immediately after the first Easter Sunday and all that is happening now through prayer. The fact that I have never physically seen an electron does not in any way shake my belief in its existence; that being so, I see no good reason why I should be unduly concerned that I have never physically seen Jesus.

Now, you might be thinking, that's all very well for one who has experienced significant changes in his behaviour resulting from prayer, but suppose one has not. Suppose, for the sake of argument, you have followed my advice, locked yourself away in the privacy of your toilet each day to pray, kept this up for two years, and yet have found no convincing evidence that you have been in contact with anyone.

Would you then be able to claim that God does not exist and Jesus did not rise from the dead?

The answer is no; a negative outcome does not count the same as a positive one. This, I hasten to add, is not because I believe my opinion carries more weight than yours! What we are dealing with here, in fact, is not a matter of opinion at all. We are not being asked to choose between like alternatives – such as voting for one political party rather than another, choosing between dresses, deciding it would be preferable to take the longer scenic route home instead of the more direct one. In instances like these, one person's opinion can indeed be as good as another's. No, the question before us is of a different sort: does something exist, or does it not? It is a question of fact, not of opinion. What we are involved in is a search. In a search, you either find what you are looking for or you do not. If you are successful, then that is the end of the matter – what you have looked for exists. But if you are unsuccessful, the outcome is less clear. Certainly one possible inference is that the object of the search does not exist. But there are others to be considered: perhaps you have looked for it in the wrong way, or in the wrong place; perhaps you were unsure as to what it would look like and so failed to recognize it; possibly you did not look hard enough. When it comes to seeking out God, I and millions of others know, from personal experience, that a negative result to the prayer experiment has to be for one of these latter reasons.

13 Attempts to Demonstrate God's Existence

In what has gone before, I have highlighted the similarities between the search for God and Jesus and the search for new properties of matter; both require acts of faith, and both make use of arguments for existence based on the ability to explain observed behaviour. But how far can this analogy be pushed? Am I claiming that there is *no* difference between religious and scientific investigation? If that were the case, an interesting possibility would arise. In scientific enquiry, there are ways of satisfactorily convincing others of the truth of an assertion without them all having to carry out the investigation for themselves. For instance, not everyone has to do the charm experiment in order to become convinced of the existence of charm. If the same were true in the sphere of religion, then there ought to be an alternative way of convincing you of the truth of the resurrection, or what amounts to the same thing for Christians, the existence of God – without you having to do the prayer experiment, or any other experiment, for yourself.

Sophocles, the fifth century Greek poet, once said: 'One must learn by doing the thing; though you think you know it, you have no certainty until you try.' In science this carries some force. I and my fellow scientists go to some pains to train our students to perform many of the classic experiments for themselves. It is good that they should learn at first hand that the physical concepts they will later be handling are rooted in experimental observations of nature. But, strictly speaking, if our concern were merely to convince them that the properties of matter we speak of exist and the scientific laws are correct, such repetition of experiments is unnecessary (which in the case of the charm experiment is just as well in view of the expense that would be incurred if everyone wanted to have a go!).

What happens is that the results of an experiment are subjected to a particularly searching kind of scrutiny. This might occur at a conference, for example. No sooner have the findings been presented than the speaker has to be prepared to defend them. Is he quite sure about his measurements? Are his instruments as accurate as he believes them to be? Is the effect he is measuring being masked by some other influence? Could his result be a statistical freak? Does he get the same result under different conditions? How do his results compare with those of other experimenters? Is the interpretation he has put on his results the only one or are there other possible explanations? And so it goes on. It is sometimes hard to believe that none of this apparent hostility is meant as a personal attack on the man himself; it is the experiment itself which is being examined and that alone.

The reason why each new result is treated so harshly and with such scepticism has to do with the pyramidal structure of scientific knowledge. Each layer of understanding is built on the one below. If a wrong experimental result or incorrect theory somehow finds its way in, then the whole structure above it becomes unsound. Einstein, whose work we shall later be considering, on more than one occasion identified faulty bricks at the very lowest levels and brought the whole edifice down! For this reason, scientists are reluctant to accept new claims until they are thoroughly tested.

The same pattern is followed when the results are later written up in the scientific journals. I have already mentioned how these accounts make for desiccated, dehumanized reading. This is quite deliberate. The writer sets out to present an unvarnished, straight account of his experimental observations; he marshalls his arguments and takes the reader in a strictly logical sequence from those observations to the inference to be drawn from them. At each point along the way, he tries to anticipate the questions and objections that his most sceptical reader might raise. In such an account, personal anecdotes, emotion and rhetoric have no place.

None of this would be possible if the results of scientific enquiry were not of a character as to lend themselves to this kind of treatment;

94

but they are. Any scientist knows that, with competence in the relevant field, he could himself repeat the experiment if he so wished. But generally, if the experiment has already been repeated a number of times, on each occasion yielding the same result, he will not consider this necessary and will be inclined to accept the observations. He will then check the logical reasoning based on the observations and convince himself of the correctness of the conclusion. In this way, he can come to accept the truth of the claim, even though he has not actively involved himself in the investigation.

So what we are asking in this chapter is whether a parallel to this exists in religious investigation. Is it possible to point to some practical observation, one that is agreed upon by all, and erect upon it a logical proof of God's existence?

None of the evidence presented so far – the evidence for the resurrection – is of that nature. Arguments based on the gospel accounts do not compel acceptance, as we have already seen; the events of Easter cannot be repeated, so there can be doubts as to whether they have been correctly reported. Neither is the experiment involving prayer admissible for the present purposes because it is one that each individual must carry out to his own satisfaction; here we are seeking the kind of proof where he has to do nothing except listen to an argument.

There have been several attempts to devise objective proofs of God's existence. One of the most famous went under the name of the *argument from design*. Briefly, this held that everything about the human body is so beautifully fitted to serve its function (with the possible exception of the appendix) that it must have been designed for that purpose. Someone must have done the designing and that someone is God – therefore, you must believe in God.

You ought not to be surprised to learn that the bottom dropped out of this argument with the development of the theory of evolution by natural selection. Our earlier discussion of Darwin's theory showed that there was an alternative way of doing the job – one that saw to it that 'poor designs' (those that did not fulfil a function well) were automatically eliminated. The evolutionary process was quite mechanical and required no Over-seeing Intelligence to direct the operations – hence the argument from design proved nothing.

Thunder and lightning were for a long time thought to be manifestations of God's wrath and consequently a proof that there was a God. This attempt to frighten people into a belief in God, for it can hardly be regarded as anything else, came to an end when Benjamin Franklin, the American scientist, flew a kite in a thunderstorm and found that a sharp metal point fixed to the kite attracted electricity to itself from the surrounding air. This showed that thunder and lightning were nothing but electrical discharges – on a grand scale to be sure, but essentially no different from what goes on nowadays in the normal household fluorescent light tube. Atheists of the time are reputed to have greeted Franklin's discovery with the claim 'God has been disarmed'. What is not so well known is that several Christians also welcomed the news; until Franklin's discovery, they had been at a loss to understand why the church towers they had built to the glory of God had so consistently been singled out for demonstrations of divine wrath! (As an aside, I would point out that lightning strikes on churches were a serious matter. In a thirty-three year period immediately following Franklin's experiment, and before the use of lightning conductors had become widespread, no less than 103 bell-ringers are on record as having been killed in thunderstorms!)

The story of what happened over the thunder and lightning argument is fairly typical. Time and again, one finds that when some natural phenomenon lacked a scientific explanation, it was attributed to divine intervention. The belief that to each effect there must be a cause led to the practice of assigning a supernatural cause to any phenomenon apparently lacking a natural one. This practice was particularly common in ancient times. In those days, there was an almost total ignorance as to why things happened the way they did: the rising and setting of the sun, the coming of rains and drought, the seasonal changes, the onset of disease, the ability to bear children and so on. The only way to 'explain' them was to attribute them to the workings of the gods. As a better understanding of the underlying processes of nature was gained, the need to invoke such gods declined.

It is the continuation of this outlook into modern times that has been characterized by the name 'God of the Gaps'. The essential feature of all such 'proofs' of God's existence is that they point to some gap in knowledge and credit the activity to the working of God. The inherent weakness of this approach is obvious: if God's role is to look after those occurrences that science cannot currently account for, it is a job without much future! Scientific knowledge continually expands and knowledge, once gained, is rarely lost. So the gaps are progressively filled and God's supposed domain correspondingly diminishes. It is not difficult to see why those who subscribe to this philosophy see in science an adversary, each advance of science marking a retreat for religion. Where will it all end? What if the relentless advance of science leads to all the gaps being plugged – and no God is found?

One might think the 'God of the Gaps' mentality belonged to the past – that it had little relevance for contemporary attitudes. I only wish this were true, but it is not. One version of it is very prevalent, its popularity being especially disturbing in view of the way scientists appear poised to expose its falsity. Adherents to this particular method of demonstrating God's existence are generally unprepared for the imminent show-down and the stage is set, so I believe, for a repetition of the same mistakes as were made over the reception of Darwin's theory. I am referring to the *argument based on the existence of life*.

Many Christians regard the subject of life – by which I mean the actual nature of life itself – as lying outside the province of scientific study. Scientists cannot produce life and never will, so it is argued. Life is a special, non-physical quality which God, and only God, can breathe into ordinary matter. It is the conclusive, tangible proof of the reality of God. Were scientists ever to refute this assertion by taking inanimate chemicals and from them producing life in a test-tube, the faith of many Christians would receive a severe jolt. It is because this question looms so large in many people's thinking, I propose we look into it rather carefully.

We begin by trying to clarify what exactly is supposed to be the difference between the living and the non-living. There is, of course, no problem in classifying human beings, cats, dogs, fish, flies and oak-trees as living, and rocks, cars, nylon shirts and the Tower of London as non-living. But when we come to simpler objects, problems arise. Yeast, for example, bought in packets at the supermarket and looking like a powder, is actually alive. Viruses, such as those responsible for the common cold, can be made into inert crystalline preparations like salt or sugar crystals, but they also reproduce, albeit in a rather

97

indirect fashion, and this makes it difficult for biologists to know whether they ought to be thought of as living or non-living.

There is no single criterion for deciding. Living matter usually exhibits various characteristics and what is important is the combination of these characteristics rather than the presence of any one of them in particular. These characteristics are *nutrition:* the ability to take in substances from the environment and use them to promote growth and provide energy for the body's activities; *growth:* with changes not only in size but also in shape; *respiration:* the process of breaking down substances in the body to release energy; *reproduction:* by either sexual or asexual means; *excretion:* the capacity to get rid of unwanted substances; *responsiveness:* the characteristic of reacting to an environment.

Inanimate objects might satisfy one or more of these criteria: a crystal of sugar will absorb chemicals out of solution and will grow larger; a lump of iron will react to a damp environment by becoming rusty. But, as we said, it is not whether a single criterion is satisfied, but the combination of all six that determines whether something is living or not. Even this requirement is not clear-cut. The viruses we mentioned earlier cannot strictly speaking reproduce themselves; what they do is infect an animal or plant and cause it to manufacture the virus material on their behalf. The fact that viruses satisfy the fourth criterion only in this indirect manner, accounts for the doubts over their status.

This lack of a neat distinction between living and non-living matter raises an interesting possibility: could we human beings have descended from chemicals? We already know that the theory of evolution traces our lineage back to ancestors that were demonstrably more primitive than ourselves. If we were to go back further in time, to an exceedingly early stage of development, what would we find – something resembling a bacterium? And even further back still, would we begin to pass through a twilight zone where our very earliest ancestors possessed only certain of the characteristics we nowadays associate with life? And finally, do we reach a point where none of the characteristics are to be found and we are in a world of plain, ordinary, inanimate chemicals such as one finds in bottles at the chemist's?

By way of answer, we first note the great strides that have been made in understanding the chemical construction of living creatures.

Molecular biology has emerged in recent years as a new field of science. It is work in this field that has led to the unravelling of the genetic code as contained in the DNA molecules. These complex molecules are now understood to be an amalgamation of smaller molecules. These in their turn are made of smaller molecules still, which are themselves made of the naturally occurring elements: carbon, nitrogen, hydrogen and so forth.

So we know the endpoint of this 'chemical evolution' process. We also have a good idea of the beginning: the conditions prevailing on the earth four or five thousand million years ago and the composition of the atmosphere as it probably was at that time. The question then is whether there exists a route whereby the gap from the beginning to the endpoint could have been spanned spontaneously through naturally occurring processes, without any need of direct divine intervention.

Experiments have shown that when an electrical discharge is sent through a mixture of gases similar to that of the primitive terrestrial atmosphere, the small molecular building blocks of living matter (amino acids and nucleotides, for instance) are duly formed. This result is of immense significance. It makes it almost inevitable that the same process took place early in the earth's history under natural conditions. The energy required for the fusion, supplied in the experiment by the electrical discharge, might have been provided by a lightning flash, or from the action of the penetrating ultraviolet light of the sun, or from naturally-occuring radioactivity, or possibly from the heat to be found near the rim of a volcano.

The next step is to get from these basic building blocks to the large molecules of biological interest (proteins and nucleic acids). How this happened is not yet clear. According to one view, the materials were accumulated in what has come to be called 'the primitive soup'. As the concentration of this solution increased with time, so the chance of the small molecules colliding and fusing to each other improved and gradually, over a long period of time, the required larger molecules were produced. The final stages of chemical evolution whereby all the necessary materials came together within a complete living cell unit is also not yet understood, though various hypotheses are currently being examined. Once the first part-living, part-non-living entities built from DNA material put in their appearance, there would have then been no further need to rely on the purely hit-and-miss processes characterizing the early stages; from this point onwards the process of evolution by natural selection would have taken over and the progress towards man and all other present-day living creatures and plants would have gathered momentum.

From what I have said, you will appreciate that scientists are still a long way from providing a definitive account of the evolution of living things from chemicals. Nonetheless, they know the beginning and endpoint and have at least gone part of the way towards bridging the gap. On the strength of this, some scientists are already claiming that it is only a matter of time before the whole picture is pieced together. This is not to say that the production of life in a test-tube is just round the corner, nor that it will necessarily happen within the lifetime of anyone living at present. But that is hardly the goal. Rather, the aim is the more modest one of devising an intellectually satisfying scenario whereby, in the distant past, life *could* have evolved from chemicals.

It is my belief that this goal will, one day, be achieved. I cannot see how anyone studying the advances made in this field in the fifty or sixty years since the modern idea of evolution from chemicals was first suggested can think otherwise. If this expectation is borne out, we shall have learnt that there is essentially a smooth gradation all the way up from a single atom to a human being, without the need at any point in the progression for a supernatural injection of a magic potion called 'life'. The concept of 'life' would thus appear as little more than a convenient collective term covering behavioural characteristics appearing at a certain level of molecular complexity. As such, the existence of life would afford no proof of God.

How do I, as a Christian, react to this possibility? Unlike many of my Christian friends who find the prospect disquieting and prefer not to think about it, I welcome it. I regard it as an enrichment of man's understanding of God and the way he goes about his work. I have never been happy with the idea of a God who creates a universe for the specific purpose of bringing into existence living creatures capable of having a loving relationship with him and yet does it in such a way that he has to suspend the normal laws governing the operation of that universe in order to inject (almost, it would seem, as an oversight on his part) the very quality of life essential to his purpose. Surely it is more gratifying to have a world run on such lines as would ensure that the smooth operation of the natural laws themselves must inevitably lead to the desired living creatures being formed in due course. That said, I have to abandon the existence of life as a proof of God. Whilst I believe responsibility for life is still ultimately vested in God, in that he puts in train the sequence of events that leads to life, he is now to be seen acting through the continuous operation of the laws rather than through their temporary suspension. But as there is no irrefutable evidence that those laws are to be attributed to God in the first place, there can be no question of anyone being compelled to believe in God merely from a study of the working of those laws.

So, the argument from life appears to go the same way as the argument from design and all other previous attempts to prove God's existence in an objective manner. The answer to the question posed at the beginning of this chapter, as to whether God's existence can be proved logically, must in my opinion be no. Though I have shown that there are important similarities between scientific and religious enquiries, there is also this difference: unless you are prepared to conduct your own individual search for God, you will not find him. Religious understanding comes not from any argument based on another's experience, but only from your own personal involvement.

It is important to recognize that this inability to demonstrate to others the truth of something known personally to oneself is by no means confined to this one matter of religious belief. It is something quite commonplace. Take, for example, a headache. Suppose you are actually experiencing a headache at this very moment. You *know* that you have a headache, but how do you convince others? How do the rest of us know that you are not just putting it on in an attempt to get out of reading any more of this book today? If you are one of those who are forever complaining of headaches, that might well be the suspicion. Or you might on some occasions get angry. You know that you are genuinely angry and so you storm and rave. But once again, how do those around you know how genuine your reactions are? For all they can tell, it might be a calculated move on your part to get your own way. Or you might be in love. You feel desolate when apart and cannot live without your beloved. Everything you say and do is perfectly consistent with what you know to be the case, namely, that you are deeply in love. But if the object of your affections is someone who has been badly let down in previous relationships with the opposite sex, you might well find that no demonstrations of affection are sufficient to break down the barriers of mistrust.

The reason we are unable to convince others of certain aspects of our experience is that, in a sense, each of us inhabits two worlds of perception. There is the world outside us, common to all and where we share the same experiences with others and, in addition, an interior world private to oneself alone. If you slam a door, for instance, that action is part of the exterior world; everyone present is agreed that you did indeed slam the door. But only you know whether you did it in anger, your anger being part of your interior world. You kiss a girl; she knows you kissed her, but she does not know whether you did it out of love, because love, too, belongs to your private world. It is the experiences of the exterior world, and those alone, that can be investigated by all and are thereby open to objective assessment. Scientific investigation is concerned with such phenomena. But experiences of the interior world cannot be so verified. No one can enter you and *become* you; they must therefore always hear of such things secondhand, from what you choose to tell them. True, if you are speaking to someone who has himself a hot temper and is always flying off the handle, he might readily believe you when you talk of the same feelings. In the same way, someone in love with the same girl as you might unhesitatingly accept that you are similarly attracted to her. But in neither case does this readiness to accept your word constitute proof and someone of a sceptical frame of mind can remain unconvinced.

The inability of others to verify, to their own satisfaction, that you do indeed have these experiences in no way diminishes their certainty for you. They are not to be classed as illusions or hallucinations (though such figments of the imagination do, of course, exist and need to be distinguished from what we are talking about). Such experiences are just as real and concrete as your perceptions of happenings in the external world.

The conviction that one has come into contact with the risen Jesus belongs to this interior world of certainties; as such it is one of the many experiences that cannot be verified from outside. But, as I have said, that is no reason for regarding it as any the less real and meaningful. Those who have had similar experiences of making contact with Jesus know what it is about and so more readily appreciate and accept others' accounts of it. But to those who have had no such parallel experience in their own lives, it is hard to understand what the experience is like, or indeed to believe that it happens at all – rather like the young boy who has yet to fall in love himself and consequently finds it difficult to make allowances for the behaviour of his elder brother in the presence of his girlfriend.

So the conclusion has to be that there is no other way of gaining proof of the living Jesus and, thereby, of the existence of God, except through personal involvement in the experiment of prayer. Unlike scientific enquiry, there is no short-cut through someone else doing the experiment for you and later convincing you by argument.

But surely, when one stops to think about it, we could hardly have expected it otherwise? If, as Christians believe, our purpose in being in the world is that we should love God, then that love has to be freely offered. Just as you cannot be argued into loving another person, so you cannot expect to be argued into a loving relationship with God.

14 The Whole is More than the Sum of its Parts

The view expressed in the last chapter that we are to be described as a pile of chemicals, devoid of any mysterious potion called 'life', is to many people distasteful and degrading. They instinctively know that there is more to them than just the stuff one buys in bottles – at least, they would like to think so. But if this is the case, how is such a claim to be justified? Where lies this certain something extra?

In 1620, Francis Bacon, the English philosopher who did much to give science its method and inspiration, enunciated the principle: 'It is better to dissect than abstract nature.' Since that time, science has progressively sought to understand the complicated phenomena around us by breaking them down into ever smaller and simpler component parts. To study the structure of the body, for example, an anatomist will dissect it and lay bare its bones, muscles, organs and so on. The cellular biologist might then take over and describe each of the anatomical components in terms of their individual cells. Next the molecular biologist sets forth the molecular structure of the various parts of the cell. Then it becomes the turn of the chemist to show how each molecule is an arrangement of atoms. The atomic physicist can explain how the individual atom is made up of tiny particles: the electrons we mentioned earlier, surrounding a central particle called the nucleus. The nuclear physicist can take the process a further stage by describing all nuclei in terms of just two particles, neutrons and protons. Finally, high energy physicists, like myself, are to be found burrowing away at the lowest strata yet uncovered, trying to understand the structure of neutrons and protons.

This process of progressively reducing everything to its component parts has been very successful. At the atomic level, for instance, one can describe not only the human body, but the whole diversity of nature with its hundreds of thousands of different chemicals, in terms of only ninety-two different kinds of atom or element. Not content with this remarkable achievement, one can then, with the help of the nuclear physicist, go on to describe even the ninety-two elements with just three basic entities: the electron, proton and neutron. This is explanatory power of an impressive order.

The success of this approach has led some to the view that this is the only way to gain knowledge. The further one goes in this direction, the deeper the understanding. The complete description consists in laying bare the object's ultimate constituents; there is nothing more to an object than the sum total of its component parts. This view is called *reductionism*. But is it right that the only kind of knowledge is that which is expressed in terms of constituents? Could there not be questions that do not lend themselves to this kind of treatment – problems that call for a different kind of understanding?

Take, for instance, the question we are currently considering: what is the nature of life? The first step of the reductionist – the insertion of the anatomist's knife – destroys the very quality we are seeking to understand. This alone gives grounds for suspecting that the type of truth revealed by reductionism might not be the only sort and the gaining of one kind of knowledge might automatically exclude one from other kinds. To appreciate the limitations as well as the successes of the search for ultimate constituents, let us look at a few examples of it in action in widely differing fields.

For instance, how would a chemist set about 'explaining' a Rembrandt self-portrait? In theory, he could draw up an inventory of all the atoms on the canvas and catalogue them according to which element they belonged and the positions they occupied. Thus he would record a cadmium atom placed next to a chromium one, which in turn was next to an atom of cobalt and so on. In practice, of course, it would be absurd to set about such a task, but that is neither here nor there – in principle, it could be done. Moreover, if we were to imagine it being done with great thoroughness, the description would be complete with nothing left out of account.

And yet it is a description that has missed the whole point of the painting. It says nothing about the old man looking at his reflection in the mirror and, in so doing, looking at us from the canvas. It does not explain why this particular arrangement of atoms strikes a sympathetic chord in us, why we recognize the pathos and resignation in that face and are led to contemplate the decay of our own youthful looks in later life, with all the emotions this stirs within us. Of such things the chemist's explanation is silent. Though the description tells us everything about the painting at the chemical level, it tells us nothing about what the painting is, why it was created and why we stand before it, touched by its sadness and yet strangely uplifted by its dignity. The description tells us both everything – and nothing.

Indeed, the further this line is pursued in the search for a description that is yet more fundamental than that offered by the chemist, the further removed one seems to become from the true essence of the painting. At the level where the nuclear physicist works, for example, one is only concerned with what goes on within the nucleus. But it is the arrangement of the electrons outside the nucleus, their distances from each other and from the nucleus itself, that determines the colour of the atom or molecule. The electrons in cadmium sulphide, for instance, are so distributed as to be able to absorb all light falling on them with the exception of the yellow component, which is reflected, and it is this that gives the pigment its yellow colour. So although the description of the painting offered by the nuclear physicist is even more detailed than that given by the chemist, it is one in which the concept of colour, surely vital to any adequate description of the essence of a painting, has now been lost.

None of this is meant to imply that the descriptions given by the chemist and physicist are invalid or do not have their uses. If a painting's authenticity is in question, it might well be desirable to call in someone with a knowledge of nuclear physics to examine it using radioactive techniques. For this purpose, it is perfectly in order to regard the painting and its canvas as a collection of nuclei, some of which might exhibit the property of radio-activity. Or again, if a painting is in poor condition, one commissions a picture restorer. His concern is with changes of colour arising from exposure to sunlight, the cracking and flaking of paint due to age and changes in humidity and the discolourations of varnish with time. For him it is important to have a knowledge of the chemistry of pigments and varnishes. Thus we see that, although unquestionably the appropriate level at which to study a painting is generally that at which the artist and the art critic operate, these other levels of description have their specialized uses.

A painting is, therefore, open to description at various levels of complexity, according to the purpose for which the description is sought. As one ascends the scale of increasing complexity, new relationships between the component parts become possible and this necessitates the formation of new concepts. We have seen, for instance, how one must rise above the level where the nuclear physicist operates before the concept of colour takes on meaning. Higher up the scale, still further possibilities arise. With a variety of molecules available, pigments can be mixed to create shades and hues, qualities not possessed by individual molecules. At a yet higher level, one can see an area of colour in relation to another and this leads to the need to introduce terms such as 'balance' and 'composition'. Finally, the picture can be considered as a whole, as a single, complete entity. It is at this level – the very opposite end to that which the reductionist process leads – that one finds the meaning and purpose of the painting.

For a second example of the strengths and weaknesses of the reductionist line of investigation, we look to music. A physicist friend of mine, who happened to be a very good violinist, had never been happy with the traditional idea that the making of first-rate violins was to be regarded as a mysterious art and that only great masters, such as Stradivarius, had the secret. He decided to apply his scientific training and reduce the process of making violins to an exact science. He began by borrowing a genuine Strad. from a musical acquaintance of his and proceeded to make a thorough analysis of the sound it produced. This was done with a standard piece of laboratory equipment called a Fourier analyser. This took each note as it was played and analysed it into its harmonic components (that is to say, tones that are twice, three times, four times, . . . the frequency of the main note). In this way he learnt exactly how much of each harmonic was present. Furthermore, he studied how the sound built up as each note was sounded, and how it subsequently died away. The combination of these features said everything there was to be said about the performance of the instrument. He knew that if he could reproduce those features exactly, then he had the equivalent of a Strad. The next step was to purchase a batch of cheap, inferior violins and modify them in such ways as to make their characteristics more closely conform to those of the Strad. Those harmonics shown by the Fourier analyser to be too weak were enhanced, others that were too prominent were damped down. At no stage in this process did he have to speak in the terms that a professional musician might when referring to the quality of the violin – the 'sweetness' of its tone, for instance. Everything had been reduced to a list of numbers that had to be matched. His approach paid off: the initially inferior violins became much improved and quite a number were sold to members of leading orchestras. (Not that they were to be reckoned on a par with a Strad. – it appears the old master still had a trick or two up his sleeve!)

What this story shows is that there is more than one way of approaching music. Just as with the Rembrandt painting, there can be a scientific description in which all its components are taken apart and laid bare. And, as we have seen, such a cold and calculating approach can have its uses. But no one would claim that the list of numbers produced by the Fourier analyser had captured the true essence of the instrument and, even less, that it had revealed its purpose. To understand that, one must enter not the laboratory, but the concert hall.

Leaving the arts, our next example of the hierarchical nature of descriptions has to do with technology. We imagine a car mechanic confronted for the first time with a new model. How does he set about getting to know it? For a start, he can study the diagrams in the garage manual – those showing all the separate components and the way they fit together. He might then take various parts of the car to pieces and examine them at first-hand. This intimate kind of knowledge is the sort that he will need later when servicing, maintaining, and repairing the car. But it is not the kind of knowledge that generally interests a prospective buyer. If one is contemplating the purchase of the car, one is unlikely to do this on the basis of what one finds in the garage manual; instead, one goes for a test-drive. As a driver, one is interested in how the car 'handles', whether the steering feels positive, how the car holds the road, the comfort of the ride, how to nurse one's way through the gears and what the fuel consumption will be. None of this information is likely to come from a study of the car's component parts. So, once again, we find that a reductionist description must sometimes be complemented by an alternative assessment based on overall characteristics.

Finally, take the case of a football team. In order for a team to make the grade, there have to be, at the basic level, endless training sessions of jogging and sprinting to build up muscle strength, stamina and speed, as well as the development of ball skills: heading, trapping, passing, shooting and running with the ball. But that is not enough. An effective team is more than a collection of players who are fit and skilful. Beyond the level of individual ability, there are team tactics and strategy, each player's efforts being seen in relation to each other's. And, at the highest level, there are yet other factors to be taken into account, such as team morale and match atmosphere. No analysis of the skills of the individual players will explain why the same players taking on the same opponents are more likely to win at home than away.

Enough of such examples. Their intention was simply to illustrate that a single phenomenon might be open to different kinds of description. Such descriptions occur at different levels of complexity and are evolved to serve specific purposes. Each makes use of its own concepts and these, whilst indispensable to one description, can be irrelevant or meaningless for another.

This is even true of purely scientific investigation. Though science continues to search for ever more fundamental descriptions, that is not to say that these lowest lying descriptions are to be regarded as necessarily 'better' than the others. Descriptions at the upper levels of complexity remain valid and will always have their uses. The division of science into biology, chemistry and physics is a reflection of this hierarchical structure. The ecologist concerned with the growth of the rabbit population in Australia has little point of contact with a physicist like myself probing the ultimate structure of matter. So there is no reason why the ecologist should not describe the world in the way that is most convenient for his purposes, using those terms and rules of behaviour that are best suited to his description. In like manner, a chemist whose job is to devise new drugs for combating disease has no need to know about the internal structure of the nucleus and so does not feel obliged to use the language and concepts of the nuclear physicist.

With these thoughts in mind then, we are ready to return to our original question – the one to do with the nature of life and the scientific description of ourselves as a pile of chemicals. Is such a mechanistic picture justified? In one sense the answer is yes – the same sense in which it was possible to describe the Rembrandt self-portrait solely in terms of chemicals. And, for a variety of purposes, it is wholly appropriate that our bodies should be regarded as nothing more than a lump of matter obeying straight-forward mechanical principles. To a physicist directing radiation at a malignant tumour, the body is just a collection of nuclei and electrons; he studies how far the radiation will penetrate into the body tissue, using the same sort of equation as he uses to investigate how far it will pass into other materials like concrete, iron or lead. The pharmacist developing new drugs to combat disease will see the body as little more than a test-tube in which chemical reactions occur. The biochemist concerned with the working of the brain and nervous system will see it as a mixture of chemicals and electrical circuits. To the surgeon, it might be a plumbing system built around a mechanical pump called the heart. To the nutrition expert, it is a machine that runs on the fuel provided in the form of food. The air-conditioning engineer will regard it as an object giving out the heat equivalent of a light bulb. To the air-craft designer, it is a weight (generally accompanied by a further twenty kilograms) that he has to get up in the air. All these viewpoints are justified and can be considered adequate at the level appropriate for answering the particular question being posed.

But none of these need, nor in fact do, have any relevance to questions concerned with what man really is and what purpose there might be to his existence. Indeed, one cannot help but notice that in all the examples we considered earlier – the painting, the violin, the car and the football team – questions to do with purpose and final aims were exclusively confined to the highest levels of complexity and organization. The same is also true of ourselves. If one is looking into the meaning to be attached to the concept of life and even more so if one is searching out the purpose of that life, whether it be in relation to God or otherwise, one cannot expect to find it at the low-lying mechanistic levels. Moreover, the deeper we delve in pursuance of the reductionist line, the further we are likely to find ourselves from the answer.

I, personally, have no objection to my fellow scientists giving a purely mechanical description of me in terms of my constituent atoms and the forces holding them together. I accept that such a description could be a complete one and thus a wholly satisfactory explanation of what I am made of and how I am put together – but only at that particular level of description. The acceptance of this description in no way prevents me from also regarding other explanations of myself, at other levels of complexity, as being equally valid and, for some purposes, more relevant. Nor does the fact that there is no need at the lower levels to refer to the concept of life mean that such a term will not come into its own at a higher level of organization. Once it is recognized that life is not to be regarded as merely a fourth constituent of matter, to be added to the other three ingredients (the electron, neutron and proton), then its absence at the atomic level is no occasion for disquiet. Rather, the term 'life' is to be seen as a concept describing the complex inter-relationships existing within certain large collections of atoms and the overall behaviour to which this gives rise.

Such a description is admittedly not very appealing, but it does set out the nature of the quality of life – at least, as I see it. The fact that the concept refers to a relationship existing between atoms does not mean that it is to be regarded as somehow less real or meaningful than, say, the individual atoms themselves. On the contrary, it can be argued quite the reverse: in the description of a human body it is *only* the relationship that matters, the individual atoms being of no consequence. The reason for this is that the material of our bodies is continually being replaced by fresh material. It enters the body as food and is broken down by the chemical processes of digestion to form new hair, skin, toenails, blood – even solid, permanent-looking bones are in a continual state of renewal. In fact, very little of the material that makes up our bodies today was there even just a few years ago, let alone when we were babies. And yet each of us experiences continuity – each remains essentially the same person throughout life. This continuity of identity cannot be vested in the atoms themselves, because these are only temporary residents of the body. The permanence lies in the way the atoms are arranged. It is the arrangement, and that alone, that gives rise to the distinctive person.

Thus the notion that there is no more to a person than the pile of chemicals that happen at any particular time to make up his body, though useful in certain limited contexts, cannot in other respects be regarded as adequate. If one is concerned with questions to do with the purpose of life, then one must consider the person as a whole, for it is only at the very highest levels of complexity that the concept of life itself takes on meaning. But this, as we have seen, points us in the very opposite direction to that of the reductionist approach. Hence any reductionist assessment of man cannot be other than misguided and inappropriate.

15 The Galileo Scandal

I want next to move on to consider the question: what *significance* are we justified in attributing to man – and not just to mankind in general, but to the individual person in particular? As a prelude, I shall begin by recalling the famous scandal involving Galileo and the church. That might seem odd at first – especially in a book primarily about the present-day relationship between science and religion. But the trial of Galileo still exerts a fascination over us today and continues to mould many people's ideas as to the nature of the church's response to scientific advance. More than that, Galileo, by his advocacy that man's home, the earth, was not at the centre of the universe, was among the first to cast doubt on traditional ideas of the status of man – ideas seemingly derived from the Bible. In the process, he triggered off a series of developments in which the place of man in the scheme of things progressively came to be seen as less and less important – developments, none of which have been more remarkable than those achieved by astronomers in our own time.

The story, as it is popularly related, goes as follows: Galileo supported the view, first expressed by Copernicus, that it was the earth that went round the sun and not the other way about. For this the church had him put on trial. He was imprisoned and subjected to appalling tortures in order to force him to recant. Having been dragged before the congregation and made to disown publicly his scientific beliefs, he then, in a last defiant gesture, rose and exclaimed 'And yet it moves!' Whereupon he was cast into the dungeons and had his eyes put out. The whole episode stands as a terrible indictment of a cruel, reactionary church, implacably opposed to enlightened scientific progress.

Whilst one is reluctant to spoil a good tale, it is only fair to point out that hardly anything of the sort actually happened! Much of the old story has now been exposed as pure legend. Historians, through gaining access to Vatican files and other letters and documents, have, over the last hundred years, pieced together a much more truthful account. What emerges, in fact, is a truth stranger than fiction. One finds, for instance, that instead of the church authorities waging an unremitting battle against the spread of the new cosmology, the Pope himself at one stage had positively encouraged Galileo to write the very book that was later to be the centre of the trouble. The book itself had actually passed the church censor before publication. So it is we are led to ask: 'What was the controversy *really* about?'

At the time of Galileo, the early part of the seventeenth century, the generally accepted cosmology was that of the Greek philosopher Aristotle (384–322 BC). He had pictured the universe as a sphere of limited size with the earth at the centre. About the earth, there were seven solid, transparent, crystalline, spherical shells arranged like the successive layers of an onion. These carried respectively the moon, Mercury, Venus, the sun, Mars, Jupiter and Saturn. There was, in addition, an outer spherical shell carrying the fixed stars. God was thought to move this outer shell and the motion was in turn communicated to the inner ones.

According to Aristotle, the spherical layer carrying the moon constituted a fundamental boundary on either side of which there operated distinct sets of laws. Below the moon there was to be found imperfection and decay. In contrast, the moon itself and the heavenly bodies beyond existed in a changeless world of perfection. Such a world-view was later, of course, to accord well with Christian philosophy, which was also to associate a perfect heaven with the higher realms.

Aristotle's ideas were subsequently elaborated by Ptolemy in about AD 150. Whilst retaining the idea that all heavenly motion must ultimately be related to the 'perfect' figure of the circle, he recognized that the motion of the planets was in fact rather complicated. Instead of moving at a steady pace across the sky like the background stars, the planets would sometimes slow down, or even stop and reverse their motion for a while before resuming their onward progress. It was to account for this irregular motion that Ptolemy introduced the idea that, instead of the planets moving in a circle about the earth, they actually moved in a circle about a point that was itself moving in a circle about the earth. The combination of these two circular motions could then reproduce the gross features of what was observed. By the introduction of further geometrical devices, which I shall not describe, the agreement could then be made even more exact.

It is important to recognize that this picture of the world was not to be regarded as mere idle speculation; it was a cosmology firmly rooted in the laws of physics prevailing at the time. According to these, the earth was 'the natural home' of heavy objects. This was demonstrated by the way all heavy objects fall towards the earth on being released and, moreover, by the manner in which the heavier ones fall faster than the lighter ones (or so it seemed). The natural state of motion of a heavy object was one of rest, as could be demonstrated by the way it required a force to keep it moving (once again, common experience *seeming* to indicate this to be the case). The earth, as the home of heavy objects, could naturally be assumed to be itself very heavy; it would therefore require a very large force to keep it moving. As no such force was in evidence, the conclusion had to be that the earth was at rest. Confirmation of this was provided by observations of the moon, the clouds, the air and the birds flying in the air. If the earth had been moving through space, there would have to be forces exerted on all these various objects in order that they should be able to keep up with the earth. There was no such force, so the earth could not be moving.

Thus the Aristotle/Ptolemy world-view of a fixed earth about which the heavenly bodies moved not only accorded well with observation but was perfectly in tune with the scientific laws of the time. The ideas of cosmology and of physics were closely interwoven and because of the beautifully self-consistent, integrated picture they presented, one can understand a natural reluctance at having this orderliness upset.

It was this same world-view that appeared to agree with a literal interpretation of certain passages in the Bible, passages seemingly indicating that the earth was fixed and the heavenly bodies moved. For example, we have:

Then Joshua spoke to Yahweh, . . . Joshua declaimed: 'Sun, stand

still over Gibeon, and, moon, you also, over the Vale of Aijalon.'
And the sun stood still, and the moon halted, till the people had
vengeance on their enemies.

You fixed the earth on its foundations, unshakeable for ever and
ever:

The sun rises, the sun sets; then to its place it speeds and there it
rises.

High above, he pitched a tent for the sun, who comes out of his
pavilion like a bridegroom, exulting like a hero to run his race. He
has his rising on the edge of heaven, the end of his course is its
furthest edge, and nothing can escape his heat.

The uniqueness of the position of the earth seemed attested not only
by such passages, but also by a general feeling that it was only right
and proper that man, being the special object of God's concern,
should occupy a home in the prime, central position; this was a view
constantly reiterated from the pulpit.

With cosmology, science and religion combining to present a united
front, it is perhaps not surprising that when Copernicus in 1543 published his theory that the sun was at the centre and immovable and
that the earth was but a planet like any other and was going around it,
hardly anyone took the idea seriously. A further reason for ignoring
his theory was that it was very complicated. Contrary to popular misconceptions of today, the Copernican theory did *not* bring about a
great simplification; on the face of it, there was little to recommend it
over the Ptolemaic hypothesis. It is true the apparent motion of the
background stars could be explained in terms of the earth rotating on
its axis. But most of the other intricate motions were still there. Indeed,
Copernicus found it necessary to call upon about twice as many circles
as Ptolemy used: he had planets going in circles about points that
were going in circles about points that were going in circles about the
sun! (No-one had yet come up with the idea of planets moving in
ellipses.)

Added to this complication, of course, was the fact that the Copernican scheme, unlike the old one, flew in the face of all known physics.

Copernicus had freely to admit that the idea that the earth rotates is 'almost in opposition to commonsense'. He was also aware that he had no answer to why the loose objects on the surface of the earth were not left behind, nor why the clouds did not progressively drift towards the west.

For these and other reasons, he foresaw that his ideas would meet with strong opposition:

> The scorn which I had to fear on account of the novelty and absurdity of my opinion almost drove me to abandon a work already undertaken.

Note that what Copernicus had to fear was not persecution by the church, but the derision of his fellow astronomers and scientists. The church itself did not take a serious interest in the matter for another seventy to eighty years. This was when a new champion of the cause came on the scene: Galileo.

Galileo, at the age of twenty-five, was already professor of mathematics at Pisa. Though it is now thought unlikely that he ever dropped objects from the leaning tower in that city, it was about this time he began his thorough-going revision of the basic laws of motion. He found that heavy objects did not fall faster than lighter ones if suitable allowance was made for the effects of air-resistance. Neither did objects require forces to keep them moving – the slowing-down commonly observed being attributable to friction. Having thus gone far towards undermining the physics upon which the Aristotelian cosmology was based, he quickly came to an acceptance of the Copernican view.

At first, he was reluctant to make his views known for the same reason as Copernicus – fear of ridicule. He wrote in a letter:

> I have written many arguments in support of him and in refutation of the opposite view – which however, so far I have not dared to bring into the public light, frightened by the fate of Copernicus himself, our teacher, who though he acquired immortal fame with some, is yet to an infinite multitude of others (for such is the number of fools) an object of ridicule and derision. I would certainly dare

to publish my reflections at once if more people like you existed; as they don't I shall refrain from doing so.

In 1609, Galileo, who by then was forty-five years old, learnt of the invention of the telescope. He built an instrument for himself and turned it upon the heavens.

The first astonishing result was that the moon was not the perfect sphere expected of heavenly bodies; it was pitted with craters and had mountains. Such imperfections were not in accord with the tenets of Aristotelian philosophy. A second observation was that Jupiter was accompanied by moons. These were seen to be going round the planet and, contrary to expectations, showed no signs of being left behind despite the absence of any agency propelling them along. This lent weight to the Copernican view that our own moon, alone among the heavenly bodies, went about the earth and was able to keep up with it as together they circled the sun. A third result was one that Copernicus himself had predicted would be a crucial test – the phases of Venus. If Venus really were circling the sun in an orbit somewhat smaller than that of the earth, then it should exhibit phases like the moon. Moreover, it should change in apparent size depending on whether it were close to the earth on the same side of the sun, or far away on the opposite side. Both these effects were clearly seen by Galileo.

Much encouraged by these results, which he took to be conclusive proof of the Copernican scheme, Galileo published his findings. His views were greeted with hostility. This stemmed mostly from his fellow university professors who felt their professional reputations had been imputed. Many refused even to look through the telescope, preferring to dismiss what Galileo had claimed to see as mere illusions generated by the dubious distorting pieces of glass in it.

The reception given by the clerics on the other hand was, on the whole, favourable. The Jesuit mathematicians of the Roman College were quickly won over and Galileo was given a cordial interview with Pope Paul V. Although some clerical figures were concerned that the authority of scripture was being called into question, Galileo's standing with the church at this time was high. This pleased him because he was a devout Catholic and was anxious to do nothing to embarrass the church. His personal conviction was that truth came both from observations of nature and also from the Bible. It was not possible for one to contradict the other. Where there were passages in the Bible apparently purporting to claim that the earth was fixed and the sun moved, these were not to be accorded a literal interpretation; instead, their true meaning had to be sought elsewhere.

It was this intrusion of a layman into theological matters that caused the Roman authorities unease. Who was Galileo to be instructing the people on how they should and should not read the Bible? What made matters worse was that Galileo was making free with these opinions at a time when the church was becoming ever more sensitive regarding its attitude towards the Bible in general. Recall that all this was happening in the aftermath of the Reformation a hundred years earlier. The Protestants having firmly asserted their adherence to the authority of the Bible rather than that of the Pope, the Roman Catholic church had become anxious to reassure the faithful of its own commitment to scripture.

The leading Protestant, Martin Luther, had already denounced the Copernican theory by appeal to scripture: 'This fool wishes to reverse the entire science of astronomy; but Sacred Scripture tells us that Josue commanded the Sun to stand still, and not the Earth.'

In the circumstances, it was not surprising that the Roman authorities were not keen to expose themselves to the accusation that they tolerated a free-and-easy attitude towards the Bible. In 1616, this unease came to a head and Galileo was summoned before the chief spokesman for the ecclesiastical position on matters of controversy. As a result of this meeting, Galileo, whilst being permitted to continue to discuss the pros and cons of the Copernican system, had in future to refrain from claiming that the theory necessarily represented the truth (and therefore by implication necessitated a reinterpretation of scripture). He should discuss the theory merely as a hypothesis. Galileo agreed to this.

Seven years later, Pope Urban VIII was elected. This caused Galileo to entertain hopes that the restriction would be lifted. He had been on good terms with the new Pope whilst the latter had still been a cardinal. The Pope had a great interest in natural philosophy and had earlier written Galileo a letter of congratulation and even a poem to celebrate the discoveries made by the telescope. Galileo thought that such an enlightened Pope would surely allow him to say whatever he wished. Soon after the election, the Pope granted Galileo several audiences. However, he did not lift the restriction – the Copernican theory had still to be spoken of as an unproven hypothesis.

Galileo was now getting on in years. His friends, together with the Pope, encouraged him to write a definitive work that would set out clearly the claims of the rival theories of Aristotle/Ptolemy and Copernicus. Accordingly, he set to and began to write his famous book *Dialogue Concerning the Two Principal Systems of the World*. It was to be in the form of a Socratic dialogue involving three participants: Salviati who speaks for Galileo in favour of the Copernican theory; Simplicio who takes the traditional Aristotelian line; and Sagredo who is (supposedly) impartial.

The Pope seemed keen on the project and not only suggested the title of the book, which Galileo agreed to adopt, but also urged him to include an argument of his own. This roughly went along the lines:

> God is all powerful and so could have established the machinery of the universe in such a way that man could never hope to penetrate its mysteries. Moreover, he could arrange things such that all the evidence pointed to one particular mechanism at work – without it actually being that mechanism at all. Thus, even if man were in possession of everything that constituted total proof of a particular mechanism, one still could not be absolutely sure that, in truth, it did correspond to reality.

Though Galileo could hardly have been enthusiastic about including such a fatuous argument, he nevertheless agreed to this as well. On completion of the manuscript, he took it to the church censor for permission to publish. The censor judged that Galileo had more or less abided by the strict letter of the restriction applied to him and had consistently referred to the Copernican theory as a hypothesis. The book received the seal of approval and it was printed in 1632. It caused a sensation. In no time all copies were sold. Everyone was talking about it.

But also in no time, Galileo was in deep trouble. Within a year of the appearance of the book he was on trial for heresy. Why? What had caused such a dramatic reversal in his fortunes? We do not have to look far for reasons.

In the first place, whilst it was true that Galileo had presented the arguments for two possible world-views, the so-called dialogue was one-sided to the point that there could only be one conclusion. Simplicio's defence of Aristotle was devastatingly torn to pieces on all counts and he himself, as the spokesman for this view, was left looking inept and foolish. All the evidence that had been marshalled supported the Copernican view: the evidence of the telescope and also additional powerful arguments concerning the cause of the tides which Galileo had recently developed. So although he had technically complied with the church ruling, it had been done in such a blatantly tongue-in-cheek manner that it was tantamount to having flouted it.

Worse was to come. The Pope, you remember, had himself asked for the inclusion of an argument of his own devising. Galileo, as we saw, complied with the request. But how tactlessly he had done it! The Pope's argument, almost word for word, was put into the mouth of the now discredited Simplicio. Having been comprehensively defeated by Salviati on all counts, Simplicio, as a last desperate act had this to say, in his closing speech, about Salviati's arguments:

I do not consider them true and conclusive; indeed, keeping always before my mind's eye a most solid doctrine that I once heard from a most eminent and learned person, and before which one must fall silent, I know that if asked whether God in His infinite power and wisdom could have conferred upon the watery element its observed reciprocating motion using some other means than moving its containing vessels, both of you would reply that He could have, and that He would have known how to do this in many ways that are unthinkable to our minds. From this I forthwith conclude that, this being so, it would be excessive boldness for anyone to limit and restrict the Divine power and wisdom to some particular fancy of his own.

To which Salviati sarcastically replied:

An admirable and angelic doctrine, and well in accord with another one, also Divine, which, while it grants to us the right to argue about the constitution of the universe (perhaps in order that the working of the human mind shall not be curtailed or made lazy) adds that we cannot discover the work of His hands.

No one at the time could have failed to recognize that the 'most eminent and learned person, before which one must fall silent' could have been anyone other than the Pope himself. Overnight Galileo had, in effect, made the Pope a laughing-stock. In so doing, he had sealed his own fate; from what is known of the character of the Pope, he was not a man with whom it was safe to take liberties.

The outcome of the trial itself was that, under a nominal threat of torture, Galileo was commanded to declare himself against the Copernican theory. I say 'nominal threat' because it was merely a form of words, it being well-known that it was illegal to torture anyone of Galileo's age. (It was this verbal threat that was later to give rise to the unfounded belief that Galileo had actually been tortured.)

Ultimately Galileo agreed to renounce his belief in the Copernican view. His famous, or rather, infamous abjuration began as follows:

I Galileo, son of the late Vincenzio Galilei, Florentine, aged seventy years, arraigned personally before this tribunal and kneeling before you, Most Eminent and Lord Cardinals Inquisitors – General against heretical pravity throughout the entire Christian Commonwealth . . . with sincere heart and unpretended faith I abjure, curse, and detest the aforesaid errors and heresies . . .

The 'Dialogue' was placed on the Index of forbidden books. Galileo was sentenced to life imprisonment and as a penance was ordered to say the seven penitential psalms once a week for three years. The sentence was commuted immediately – indeed it was set aside before it had even been signed and ratified by the Pope. The fact that he was formally sentenced, of course, later gave rise to the subsequent stories of Galileo languishing in prison. In truth, he never saw the inside of a prison. He was not even lodged there for the duration of the trial, living instead in a comfortable five-room suite with a servant provided to look after his needs. In the end, he was even excused the necessity of saying the penitential psalms, his daughter, a Carmelite nun, being permitted to say them for him.

I have dealt with the case of Galileo in some detail. This, I think is justified because it is only right that the record be put straight. In the first place it has to be admitted that the church still emerges from the episode with little credit, but at least the picture is not as black as it is usually painted. Secondly and more importantly, we see that the incident was not the big Science v. Religion confrontation some people would have us believe, but rather a petty and inconsequential squabble. By far the dominant motivation behind the trial was something that appears nowhere in the charges – the Pope felt personally betrayed, tricked and insulted by a former friend. Galileo was himself in no doubt that this was what the trial had really been about. Years afterwards he was to write in a letter:

I hear from Rome that His Eminence Cardinal Antonio and the French Ambassador have spoken to His Holiness and attempted to convince him that I never had any intention of committing so sacrilegious an act as to make fun of His Holiness, as my malicious foes have persuaded him and which was the major cause of all my troubles.

I am of the opinion that Galileo never intended deliberately to ridicule the Pope; rather it was his enthusiasm for the Copernican theory that ran away with him. I feel also it would be wrong to lay the blame wholly on the Pope. He had been placed in an invidious position; quite apart from feeling personally insulted, he had to take into account that many interpreted Galileo's action as a deliberate affront to the headship of the church. Though he might have overlooked a personal embarrassment, he could not ignore what was considered to be a slight on the dignity of his office.

Looking back, it is easy to see that the incident should never have been allowed to happen. As we considered at length when discussing the reception given to Darwin's theory of evolution, certain passages in the Bible were never intended to be taken as literally true. One should have no more tried to deduce from those passages quoted earlier that the sun moves, than one would from references made in our post-Copernican world to the sun 'rising' and 'setting' and 'going behind a cloud'. So, even if the controversy had genuinely been about the subject of the official charges laid against Galileo, it was an embarrassing nonsense.

Fortunately, the church does seem to have learnt a lesson. These days it is inclined to walk more circumspectly where scientific matters are concerned. Recently, in response to calls for a ban on the works of the modern scientist-cum-theologian, Teilhard de Chardin, Pope Pius XII declined with the wry comment: 'One Galileo in two thousand years is enough.'

16 The Significance of the Individual

With the removal of the 'Dialogue' from the Index in 1822, the Galileo affair was, at last, brought to an official close. The Copernican theory was acknowledged to have won the day; the argument was over. But the discoveries of Galileo left a legacy: the uncomfortable feeling that the status of man was not what it had earlier been assumed to be.

The realization that the earth was only a planet much like any of the others circling the sun, was later to be followed by the disclosure that there was not even anything particularly special about the sun; it was a medium-sized star occupying an undistinguished position about two-thirds of the way out from the centre of our galaxy. The galaxy itself was also quite ordinary, no different from any other. The victory for Copernicus then, was not the end of the matter; it marked only a beginning. Aristotle's crystalline, spherical shells having been breached, the telescope was to thrust the horizons further and further back, each new revelation displaying ever greater stretches of space.

Confronted with such immensity, it is hard to believe that so vast a place has been designed specifically to accommodate man – or even, for that matter, all of life in what one presumes to be its many forms throughout the universe. Some see here another attack by science on religious belief. They hold that the kind of universe revealed by science is out of keeping with the basic requirements for creating and sustaining life. The observed disparity argues against any would-be religious interpretation of the relationship between life and the universe; life is rather to be seen as an accidental by-product.

By way of answer, we first note that for life to put in an appearance, phenomena on a surprisingly large scale have to take place. The bulk of the material making up our bodies – the carbon, oxygen and nitrogen atoms, for example – was not present in the early stages of the universe. Out of the Big Bang, there emerged only the two lightest kinds of atom, hydrogen and helium. On condensing to form stars, these underwent nuclear reactions to produce the heavier types of atom. Some of the stars exploded, emitting the newly formed atoms into space. These atoms were later incorporated into stars of the type to which our sun belongs and into planets – and eventually into ourselves. So the stuff out of which our bodies are made originated in the fiery interior of exploding stars. In order to produce a man, first make a star! And stars have to be big; they need to contain a lot of matter in order to give rise to sufficient gravitational attraction to hold the system together whilst the violent nuclear reactions take place. The production of stars requires a great deal of gas to come from the Big Bang in order to have enough of an inhomogeneity in its otherwise uniform distribution to act as a centre upon which the material can condense. The evolution of living creatures, therefore, necessarily involved processes on a vast scale. Whether the universe had to be quite as big as it is though, I would not like to say.

It is also relevant to point out that modern science has more to say about the universe than the simple statement that it is big. In recent years, cosmologists have come to understand much about the early stages of the universe's history; they can even shed light on what happened in the first few minutes following the Big Bang. One discovery is that, for life to have subsequently put in an appearance, the early conditions had to be just right. If the expansion had been slower, the gravitational attraction between the matter of the universe would have eventually halted the expansion and pulled all the material back together again – and this could have happened too quickly for any stars to have had a chance to form. Stars would also not have formed if the expansion had been faster; in this case the expansion would have dispersed the material too rapidly for condensation to occur. Between these extremes lies a narrow band of conditions in which our universe is to be found. Of course, if conditions had been otherwise, we would not be here to contemplate our non-existence! But that is beside the point. What matters is that we do exist and, on the assumption that there is only one universe, it is very odd that it should have been so finely tuned to meet our needs. Our existence not only depended upon there being a planet like the earth – the whole universe had to be started off in just the right way. A mere coincidence? Perhaps. But then again it might be indicative of some deeper reason.

But, in any case, none of this kind of argument is necessary in order to establish a religious dimension to the relationship between man and the universe. An entirely different way of looking at things, and one I prefer, is to recognize that the universe is more than just a place for man to live. According to Christian belief, the universe fulfils a second function: 'The heavens declare the glory of God, the vault of heaven proclaims his handiwork.' Through creation, God gives expression to himself – he not only satisfies our own basic needs but reveals to us something of his own splendour. What modern science has shown is that the kind of universe we live in more faithfully reflects the nature of God than it does our own minimal requirements.

Whilst it might be true that the findings of astronomy do not necessarily devalue the significance of life – that is to say, life considered in its entirety throughout the cosmos – surely, one might think, it must affect how we view ourselves as individuals. Set against the teeming multitudes of life-forms populating outer space, can you or I any longer regard ourselves as having any significance? Where now stands the Christian assertion of the supreme worth of the individual?

This argument has not only emotive power but undoubtedly some merit. As far as the running of the universe is concerned, we as individuals count for nothing. If you or I were to die, or indeed had never existed, the main features of the universe would remain the same – the galaxies would still be there and the life they support would continue unchanged.

There is nothing new in this. We have no need to speculate about life on other planets to sense our own lack of consequence for the development of life in general; the number of Chinese alone is as near infinity as makes no odds (I even get this feeling of being overwhelmed by numbers when shopping in London's Oxford Street). Admittedly, a few people – Caesar, Napoleon, Hitler – gain prominence of sorts, but their influence is transitory. As for the rest of us, even so brief an hour in the limelight is denied us. No, there is no escaping the fact that you and I are insignificant not only on the cosmological scale, but also in regard to life here on earth.

It is only when we lower our sights – to the level of the family or a close circle of friends – that the assessment of our importance undergoes a change. As a father or mother, husband or wife, son or daughter, or best-friend, we can begin to see ourselves as assuming a place of consequence in the lives of others. It is only a limited kind of significance to be sure, but real nonetheless.

The fact that our close acquaintances are alone in recognizing our worth does not, of course, mean that they are any different from those who do not. They are simply the ones who happen to have come into contact with us. Had circumstances been otherwise, it would have been a different set of people who would have got to know us and who would by now be showing interest and concern in us. So, in addition to being of actual consequence to those who happen to be around us, we are potentially of consequence to a much wider circle of people.

Occasionally, this potential of the individual to arouse interest in almost anyone is given a chance to manifest itself. A little girl, for instance, might go missing from home; newspapers take up the story with banner headlines and in no time everyone seems to be concerned about her. The popular press thrives on 'human interest' stories such as these.

A different example of the power of the individual to evoke a response came up recently at my local church. We had been trying to raise some money to help with the education of children in developing countries. Our attempts had not been very successful so we abandoned the general appeal and tried a different approach. Under the new scheme, ten people were to band together to provide the money for the schooling of a specific child. The contributors would receive regular school reports and letters from 'their' child and so be kept informed of his or her progress. The idea caught on and, in the end, several teams of contributors were formed to finance a number of children in different parts of the world.

It is the personal angle that is again emphasized in the TV and radio soap operas. These highly popular programmes are not about exciting events or great people. Instead, they concentrate on thoroughly routine occurrences as they affect ordinary men and women. The success of these series hangs on the degree to which they mirror real life and, accordingly, the ease with which the audience can identify with the characters and share in their problems.

The fact that perfectly ordinary people are capable, at least potentially, of arousing wide interest, should occasion no surprise. Considered in isolation, the typical human being is a remarkable phenomenon: a rich amalgam of thoughts, hopes, aspirations, insights, past experiences, emotions, powers of reasoning, ability to love – all contained within a physical body of breathtaking intricacy and beauty. Each of us is a creature of remarkable complexity and profundity and, as the Bible puts it, 'fearfully and wonderfully made'. That being so, why do we continue to think of ourselves as lacking significance?

The reason has to do with what we understand by 'significance'. To be able to regard ourselves as significant, it appears we need to be convinced not only that we possess intrinsic worth and are potentially an object of concern and interest to others, but also that such potential is actually realized and our worth universally recognized. It is in this latter respect that the numbers argument comes into its own; in a world as populous as ours, recognition beyond the immediate circle of acquaintances becomes a physical impossibility.

But, whilst accepting that true significance does require intrinsic worth to be recognized, is it really the case that our self-esteem and dignity should hinge on winning the attention of our fellowmen; is it necessary that we leave our mark on the world? The Christian answer is no. To the Christian mind, it is immaterial whether we are known to many or to only a few. Our intrinsic worth is already fully recognized and acknowledged – by God. Unlike ourselves, God is not subject to physical limitations. He is present everywhere, at all times, simultaneously devoting his attention to us all, each as individuals. It is through God our potential worth is realized and becomes an actuality. It is through him we become significant.

All very well, but to many, such a belief is nonsense. It flies in the face of the laws of nature – and in a manner far more serious than the performance of any miracle. A miracle, as we saw, is a temporary suspension of the normal rules governing the behaviour of the world. As it is possible to imagine a universe run on different lines to our own, there does not appear to us to be anything particularly sacrosanct about the rules governing its behaviour and we can readily accept that they could, theoretically, be flouted. Whether in practice they are flouted is another matter; we are free to make up our own mind on that score, it being possible neither to prove nor to disprove that miracles actually do occur. But God being everywhere, at all times, attending to everyone as individuals, appears to confront us with a state of affairs that is impossible – not merely improbable or unusual, the subject of discussion and personal belief – but demonstrably, logically, impossible. Does not commonsense establish that this simply *cannot* happen?

17 God in Space and Time

Questions about God almost invariably contain within them some underlying assumption about the nature of space and time: 'When and how did God come into existence?'; 'What lies outside the universe and who created *that*?'; 'Where is heaven?'; 'What happens when it's full?'; 'Won't it be boring doing the same thing for eternity?'; 'How can God know what I shall do before I have done it?' These questions, together with the problem posed at the end of the last chapter, are but a sample. Each of them arises from a simplistic extension of everyday thinking: heaven is thought of as a place much like any other and so has to be located somewhere; the universe is regarded as positioned somewhere in space, instead of being that which establishes the space; creation is thought of as an event that happens in time like all other events, rather than that which marks the beginning of time.

'Commonsense' notions of space and time are so deeply woven into our thinking that we are barely aware of them. They are assumptions of the seemingly obvious. But, in fact, they are not obvious at all. Scientists this century have subjected them to close scrutiny and exposed almost all of them to be *false*. Though our familiar notions of space and time might be adequate for the description of everyday objects and routine happenings – the context in which they were originally developed – they fail under conditions of extreme speeds, heavy masses, vast spaces or tiny distances. In such circumstances, possibilities previously thought of as inconceivable become a reality.

Not that the man-in-the-street is aware of this and there is no particular reason why he should be. As I have said, the old ideas remain good enough if all one is concerned about is living out one's day-to-day life. But this lack of awareness of the revelations of modern physics will not suffice if one is interested in questions of a fundamental nature. If our usual thinking about space and time cannot cope with the out of the ordinary but still purely physical phenomena to be found in the laboratory and in the far reaches of the cosmos, we must surely be on our guard when applying them to a sphere that goes beyond that which is merely physical – the realm where we have the temerity to attempt an explanation of God's behaviour.

Too often, in the past, man's thoughts about God have been small-minded. Ancient attempts to describe the behaviour of the gods appear to us amusingly naive. The old gods were little more than overblown, larger-than-life human beings or variants of animals equipped with a few magical tricks. Their ways were often inscrutable, but in no different a sense to the way our own behaviour might strike others as unpredictable and dependent on our mood. In essence, these gods could be understood by the mind of man; this, we now recognize, was because they were only products of the mind of man.

Such criticism cannot easily be levelled at the God of Christianity. Here we are dealing with a god that does not allow of any simple explanation. The more one studies the Christian conception of the divine, the more subtle and complex it is found to be. There is something impenetrable about it. It is as though one comes to a frontier of the knowable: beyond lies that which, to the human mind, will never be completely understood. This is how it should be. God, as we must expect, is all that we are and more besides. By 'more' I mean not only bigger, better, or more powerful, but also 'more' in the sense of being different – different in some fundamental way that borders on the unimaginable, the unthinkable.

Integral to the Christian conception of God is the way he is thought to relate to space and time. Though this relationship does not conform in all respects to the requirements governing physical objects – nor should it – it is found to have more in common with the enriched vision offered by modern physics than it does with the narrowly confining limitations imposed by the view derived from everyday experience. Any sensible approach to those apparently worrying questions about God and heaven must, therefore, be made with some knowledge of the modern view of space and time. This is not to say that I am about to reveal the answers to those questions. On the contrary, what I think modern physics does is provide reasons for believing that questions derived on the basis of outmoded ways of regarding space and time have no answers at all; despite making grammatical sense and sounding like reasonable questions, they are in fact devoid of meaning. To see how this comes about we need to take a look at Einstein's theory of relativity.

But first, a few words of reassurance might be in order! For all I know, you might be one of those who regard the theory of relativity as science at its most difficult and baffling. To hear some people talk, you would think that only geniuses on a par with Einstein himself could ever hope to understand it. This is far from true. But it is only fair to acknowledge that relativity does pose its problems and represents something of a departure from the kind of science we have until now been considering. The topics we have touched on so far – mostly evolution, astronomy and a bit about atoms – have been comparatively straightforward. Admittedly, it was difficult to gain a true feeling for the magnitude of some of the quantities involved – the vast number of stars, or the smallness of atoms – but there is no fundamental problem in understanding what is meant by 'a lot of stars' or by 'a very tiny distance'. On coming to the work of Einstein, however, we are faced with a challenge of a different nature. Einstein undermines the very processes upon which our thinking is based. It is not a question of our having to extrapolate our present thinking to encompass larger or smaller scale phenomena; rather, we have to go back to the drawing board and examine the meaning to be attached to the very words and concepts we customarily take for granted and the assumptions in which our reasoning is rooted – assumptions that until now we have regarded as commonsense. As Einstein once mischievously remarked: 'Commonsense merely consists of those layers of prejudice laid down in the mind before the age of eighteen.'

Our approach to peeling off those layers of prejudice will not be through a physics lesson – at least, I hope what follows will not strike you as such. There will be no attempt to justify Einstein's conclusions through an examination of his arguments, nor, of course, will there be any mathematics. Instead, I shall content myself with stating his conclusions without proof. This will be sufficient for our purposes, because all I want you to get from the discussion is a general impression – that is all – just an impression of the new understanding of space and time. So, to the non-scientists I say: Take courage! You might well have to read the ensuing pages more slowly and carefully than is your custom – the material they contain is certainly not of a sort that can be skimmed through lightly. But provided you are prepared to approach the physics step by step, you ought to be able to make some sense of it.

Before setting out the conclusions of relativity theory, let me tell you how Einstein initially came to consider such matters and what led him to realize that there was something fundamentally wrong. His thoughts began with a simple observation, obvious to anyone who has stopped to think about it: when travelling at a steady pace in a straight line it is impossible to tell that one is on the move. On board an aircraft or train, there is, of course, some lack of steadiness and the engine vibration or bumpiness in the ride gives the game away. But, apart from these, we eat, read, sleep and generally conduct our lives in the same way as someone who is stationary. Einstein latched onto this idea and gave it a name; he called it his Principle of Relativity. This principle states that the laws of nature are the same for two people in steady uniform relative motion. Though this might seem a pretty innocuous statement, Einstein recognized that it was not so. He noticed that one particular law of nature, familiar to all physicists at the time, did not appear easily to fit in with his principle. This law predicted a value for the speed of light. Though we customarily think of light as travelling instantaneously from one place to another, in fact it travels at a fast but well-defined finite speed: 186,000 miles per second. This value is the one predicted by the law. Now, if Einstein's principle holds for all laws of nature, including this one, then it has a most peculiar consequence.

Suppose there are two men travelling relative to each other; one might be stationary on the ground, the other flying overhead in an aircraft. If they both look at a light pulse then the law tells them that the pulse travels at 186,000 miles per second relative to each of them. This must be so because Einstein's Principle of Relativity says the law applies equally to both of them and the law only comes up with one value for the speed of light. But that is odd – speeds do not normally behave like that. If, instead of looking at the light pulse, they were both to observe, for example, the drinks trolley being trundled up the aisle to the front of the aircraft, they would come to different conclusions about the speed of the trolley. According to the passenger in the aircraft it might be moving at a leisurely two m.p.h. But for the man on the ground, if he sees the aircraft flying past him at 600 m.p.h., the speed of the trolley in the aircraft will be 602 m.p.h. – for him the two speeds must be added to get the total speed of the trolley relative to him. So the speed of the trolley relative to a person observing it depends upon his own motion. Not so, the speed of a light pulse. Unlike any other object in nature, light has a speed that is governed by a physical law and because this law is subject to the Principle of Relativity, it must be valid for everyone regardless of their motion; a light pulse must, therefore, be seen to travel equally fast regardless of whether it is viewed from the ground or from the aircraft. This conclusion ran contrary to the prevailing ideas of the time. Before Einstein, it had been assumed that the figure of 186,000 miles per second applied only to stationary persons and anyone on the move would have to make due allowance for their own motion.

Experiment came down firmly on the side of Einstein. The speed of light has been repeatedly measured under a variety of circumstances – some where the source of light moved and others where the person making the observation moved. Always the result is the same: 186,000 miles per second. The speed of light is unique just as Einstein thought it should be.

So what is the implication of this discovery? It is not the obvious one – that there is something 'peculiar' about light; the significance goes deeper. What has been called into question is our understanding of the concept of speed and the way speeds behave, that is to say, the way they add together. But what is speed? It is simply the distance travelled in a given time. So a revision of the concept of speed must necessarily imply a corresponding revision of the underlying ideas about distance (i.e. space) and time. It was in this way that Einstein was motivated to develop his theory of relativity – undoubtedly one of the finest achievements of the human mind.

But as promised, I shall now skip the detailed mathematical

arguments and simply present you with the results of relativity theory. All that I shall now describe can be shown to follow from the acceptance of the uniqueness of the speed of light as a fact of nature – a fact demonstrated by experiment.

According to relativity theory, the normal laws of motion are to be regarded as only approximations to the truth. To be sure, their accuracy at the speeds encountered in day-to-day life is of a very high order and this, together with the fact that their formulation is reasonably simple, ensures that they are still widely taught and used today. But they are, nevertheless, only approximations to their more accurate and complicated relativistic counterparts. In the example we gave of the trolley in the aircraft, the figure of 602 m.p.h., arrived at by the straightforward expedient of adding together the speeds of the trolley and aircraft, is perfectly adequate and we have no need to be unduly concerned that the true value, according to the proper relativistic method of calculation, is a little less: 601.999 999 999 998 m.p.h. But at higher speeds, approaching that of light, the discrepancy becomes more noticeable, the combined speed dropping further and further below the value obtained by adding the two independent speeds. Ultimately, one finds that if one is dealing with light (so that one of the two speeds to be added is the speed of light itself) then the combined speed is no different from the uncombined speed, the light pulse appearing to travel equally fast for both the passenger in the aircraft and the person on the ground.

It can be shown that a direct consequence of this is that time as experienced by an aircraft traveller (the time he uses to judge the speed of the light pulse) is not the same as time experienced by the stationary person. The traditional idea that time is absolute – that it marches on at a steady pace and is the same everywhere and for everybody – must be abandoned. To see what this means, imagine an astronaut travelling in an ultra-advanced rocket capable of going at speeds comparable to that of light. Were he to go on a long journey, he would discover on his return, that he had aged less than his colleagues who had been left behind! If, for instance, he had a twin brother who had opted to become a mission controller at Houston rather than an astronaut like himself, their ages would get out of step – he would now be the younger of the two brothers. At higher speeds, the effect becomes more marked;

in particular, were he to attain the speed of light itself, he would not age at all – for he accomplishes the journey in no time at all.

Rockets travelling at such speeds are, of course, still in the realms of science fiction; the effect we are talking about though, is real enough and has been experimentally confirmed. An extremely precise clock (one using atomic vibrations to control its time-keeping) has been flown in an aircraft and compared with an identical one kept stationary on the ground. It was found to lag behind the other by just the amount Einstein would have predicted for the particular speed at which the aircraft flew. An even more convincing experiment was one in which radio-active sub-atomic particles were made to travel at a speed which was only a fraction of a per cent less than that of light. It was found that the rate of the radio-activity slowed down by a factor of thirty compared to normal – once again exactly what Einstein would have predicted in the circumstances.

Not that this has anything to do with the long sought secret of eternal youth. Though it is true an astronaut travelling as fast as those radio-active particles would age only one year if his journey had seemed to us on earth to have taken thirty years, his own experience of life would not have been in any way abnormal; to him time would not have appeared to drag. With everything happening in the rocket at a slow pace – the rate of the clocks, his heart-beat, his breathing, thinking and perception – life to him would appear to be proceeding at a perfectly normal rate. A clock going thirty times slower than normal, examined by a brain that is also ticking over thirty times slower, is perceived to be keeping normal time. There is nothing aboard the space-craft to provide an absolute standard of time against which the astronaut can make a comparison. This is not because all the bodily processes and all the equipment happen to be malfunctioning in the same way, or anything of that kind. It is time itself that is being affected. Time, as we said, is not absolute – it is relative.

That was the first example of our commonsense notions of time being overturned. The second is equally startling: two people in relative motion do not agree on whether two events occurring at different locations happen at the same time or not. Suppose, for example, synchronized time signals are broadcast from two radio stations, one in London, the other in Manchester. According to the broadcaster, they were both emitted to coincide exactly with twelve o'clock mid-day. To a high-speed astronaut passing overhead, the situation would not appear that way. If travelling north, he would regard the signal from London to have been broadcast a little later than that from Manchester; if he had been travelling south, he would have reached the opposite conclusion – the one from London was broadcast first. The amount by which the broadcast times differ would depend upon his speed, the lack of synchronization being noticeable only when his speed approached that of light. The effect is no illusion; the astronaut is making no mistake, his observations are not at fault, neither has he incorrectly calculated the allowances he must make for the finite time it takes for the signals to travel from the transmitters to his receiver. The effect arises because time for the astronaut is not the same as time for the stationary broadcaster. So we find that the decoupling of one person's time from that of another leads not only to there being differing rates, but also to events that are simultaneous for one not being simultaneous according to the other.

We turn next to the properties of space. Are these also affected by relativity? We can answer that fairly easily in the following way. Two people in relative motion will agree on their relative speed. The mission controller sees the astronaut's space-craft leaving him at the same speed as the astronaut sees the earth receding from him. But speed, as we have said, is the distance travelled in a given time and the astronaut and mission controller do not agree about time. So how can they agree about the speed? The answer is they also disagree about the distance travelled. If the journey lasts thirty years according to the controller and only one year according to the astronaut, then the latter concludes that at the agreed speed he must have travelled only one thirtieth of what is usually regarded as the distance from the earth to the star he visited; according to him the star is closer. Motion there-fore not only stretches out time, it also contracts space.

Remarkable though these observations on differing times and dis-tances might be, even more thought-provoking is the conclusion to which they point. Close examination of the way these variations be-have allows us to trace them back to their source: the fact that we inhabit a world that is not three-dimensional, as we are accustomed to think, but four-dimensional. To understand what this means, one really ought to go into the mathematics of the subject. This we clearly cannot do. Instead, I shall give an analogy.

Imagine I am holding up a pencil in front of a projection lamp so that it casts a shadow on a distant wall. As I rotate the pencil, the length of the shadow varies; it looks long when the pencil is illuminated broadside-on and short in the end-on position. Despite these changes in the length of the shadow, however, the length of the actual pencil itself, of course, remains the same. The fact that an object existing in three dimensions gives differing two-dimensional projections according to the viewpoint chosen is something we readily understand.

We now treat this as an analogy. Relativity tells us that three-dimensional distances vary according to one's viewpoint (which means, in relativity, according to one's speed). Could it be that the three-dimensional distance is only a projection – a projection of an 'object' that actually exists in four dimensions? If so, we might find that in spite of differences in the three-dimensional projections, distances measured in four dimensions are the same regardless of viewpoint. This turns out to be the case. The four dimensions involved consist of our normal three spatial dimensions, but now supplemented by a fourth. This fourth dimension is very closely associated with what we understand to be time. The four-dimensional 'object' is the separation between two events. One event might be the moment of launching of a rocket from earth, the other its subsequent arrival at a star. Though astronaut and mission controller disagree both about the spatial separation of the two events (the distance between the earth and the star) and also about their temporal separation (the journey time) they do agree over their separation in four dimensions.

The concept of four dimensions defies the imagination. I mean that quite literally; we cannot form a mental image of it because our brains are not made to work that way. As far as mental pictures are concerned, once one has up-down, left-right and backward-forward, we have exhausted the possibilities and there seems no other direction in which to go! This is where mathematics comes to the rescue. Physicists do not need to use analogies; through their mathematical equations they are able to explore the properties of four dimensions as easily as three. What the mathematics of relativity reveals is that space and time are inextricably linked together in a way that had never previously been appreciated.

Einstein did not let the matter rest there. Extraordinary though his achievements had already been, he regarded this as only a beginning. When he later incorporated into his theory the effects of gravity, he discovered that yet further modifications to space and time were required. Not only is it necessary to think of a four-dimensional space-time, but one that can be affected by the presence of gravitational matter. One consequence of this is that, close to a massive body such as the sun, the shortest distance between two points is no longer a straight line but a curve (hence the expression sometimes used: 'curved' space-time). This raises an interesting possibility: it concerns the overall curvature of space-time produced by the sum total gravitational attraction of all the matter in the universe. This global effect could give rise to a universe that was finite in size (i.e. did not go on for ever and ever into space) and yet at the same time had no edge, that is to say it would have no boundary beyond which anything else existed. Once again this is a topic that cannot be dealt with adequately in a non-mathematical way. However, in view of its direct relevance to one of the questions posed at the beginning of this chapter – the one to do with what lies outside the universe – let me say a brief word about it with the help of a second analogy.

Think of a small insect crawling about on a very large surface. It starts off from a certain point with the intention of crawling in a straight line until it reaches the edge of the surface. Our intrepid explorer travels on and on, supposing all the time that it is getting further and further away from its starting point and correspondingly closer to the edge. Imagine its surprise when, suddenly in front of it, there is the point from which it set out! How did this happen? There is really no mystery: the surface was not flat – it was the surface of a rather large balloon. So, although the insect had kept to a straight line within the two-dimensional surface, the curvature in the third dimension (of which it was unaware) had the effect of bringing it back to its starting-point.

We now extend this idea. Instead of an insect moving on a two-dimensional surface, we have an astronaut moving in three-dimensional space. He leaves the earth in his rocket aimed in a given direction.

He continues in a straight line with the intention of reaching the edge of the universe. Suddenly, ahead of him: the earth! This seemingly bizarre outcome is now regarded by physicists as a perfectly serious possibility. They know that the matter of the universe (contained in the galaxies and in the various forms of radiation passing through space) will tend to curve four-dimensional space-time. The extent of the curvature will depend on the amount of matter. If there is sufficient, then the universe will close back on itself and give rise to this unusual round-trip journey. Under these conditions, the universe would have a finite size (the actual size depending on how far the astronaut has to travel in a straight line in order to find himself back at his startingpoint), but there would be no boundary to cross. In such a universe one could journey ceaselessly and never come to an edge – there would be no 'outside'.

I could talk indefinitely about the work of Einstein, but I have probably already said enough to give you a feel for what it is like to glimpse the world through his extraordinary mind. You should now have some understanding of why I say that modern science has undermined almost all our customary assumptions concerning space and time. Though, as I said earlier, none of this has much relevance for the way we live our ordinary everyday lives (because we rarely come across conditions where our normal rough-and-ready ideas of space and time are not good enough), a physicist probing the deepest secrets of the physical world has no alternative but to look upon space-time from the standpoint of relativity; for him it is essential that he be aware of the true nature of space-time and the range of possibilities that have now been opened up.

If this is so for the physicist as he studies the physical world, the same must surely apply to ourselves as we enquire into the nature of God and the manner in which he operates in space and time. The questions we ask should be at least as profound as those asked by the physicist. Indeed, they need to be more so, for we seek to go beyond that which is merely physical.

With this in mind, let us take a look at some of those questions we posed earlier – the ones to do with God and heaven. We do this, remember, not with the intention of looking to relativity theory to provide the answers. Rather, it is in order to examine their underlying assumptions concerning space and time and to see how they measure up to the new possibilities allowed by the latest physical theories.

For a start, there are those questions to do with heaven. Even if it were a place like any other and in need of a physical location of some sort, which I doubt, I cannot see this as a problem. Our thinking now goes beyond three dimensions. The reason it took so long for the fourth dimension to be recognized has to do with the way it is perceived differently from the other three. Could this be taken to mean that there might be a fifth dimension perceived even more indirectly? (At the time of writing, there actually is a serious suggestion among physicists that there is such a fifth dimension and that it might have something to do with the existence of electric charge – but this for the present, is only speculative.) How about a sixth and a seventh dimension? Could there be dimensions lying entirely beyond our perception – containing universes, the existence of which we must forever remain ignorant – dimensions that perhaps contain heaven? As for the idea that heaven would be boring, with everyone playing endlessly on their harps, surely this does not remain a worry when we now know that an astronaut travelling at the speed of light (and so slowing down his time processes to a standstill) would require all of eternity to strike a single note!

Then there are questions that imply that God can transcend time – for example, his knowing what is going to happen before it actually has happened. Whereas for us, time is perceived instant by instant in a strictly sequential fashion, God is presented as someone to whom all of time – past, present and future – is known. Though this seems to us almost incomprehensible, does that mean it is necessarily impossible – logically impossible? By way of an answer, let me first ask you whether you have ever stopped to think how odd it is that we willingly accept the notion that all of space is in existence at each point in time and yet we tend not to regard all of time as being 'in existence' at each point of space? It clearly has something to do with the difference in the ways in which we perceive space and time. But that is not to say that our way is the only one. An important result of relativity is that it has revealed hitherto unsuspected similarities between space and time. Instead of being distinct and independent of each other as previously thought, space and time are now recognized as being integrally bound up with each other in an enlarged 'space' of four dimensions. Though this does not mean that time has now to be regarded as identical in every respect to the three spatial dimensions – it clearly is not – one is, nevertheless, led to enquire how close the similarities might be and the extent to which the roles of space and time might be interchanged. In this way, it becomes legitimate to ask why one should only regard the whole of space as being 'in existence' and not the whole of time. This thought comes home to me with particular force when, in my work on relativity, I have to draw what are called 'space–time diagrams'. These are diagrams where one plots time along a vertical axis and one of the spatial dimensions along the horizontal axis. A point on this diagram represents a particle at a specific point in space at a particular point in time. The line connecting up all the points on the diagram relating to the particle's position at successive times represents, at a glance, the whole history of the particle and the way its position changes with time. For any chosen point on the line, that part of the line below the point represents the positions it occupied in the past, whilst the part above the point represents its future positions. Looking down on such pictures and seeing the particle's past, present and future all on display often makes me wonder if this is what God's perception of space and time might be like. It certainly tends to make one reluctant to adopt the dogmatic view that such a vantage point is impossible.

Then there are questions to do with creation and what might have happened or existed before that moment. One of the consequences of Einstein's later work was that the matter in the universe – the galaxies – ought to be on the move, either rushing away or coming together. Astronomers confirm that the galaxies are in fact moving apart. This is taking place in the aftermath of the Big Bang, which is presumed to be the moment of creation. But is this necessarily so? Was the universe really created at the instant the Big Bang was initiated?

By way of answer, we note that one theory currently being studied by cosmologists is that the present stage of expansion of the universe will not last for ever. Although the galaxies are moving apart, their rate of separation is slowing down due to the gravitational attraction between them tending to pull them back together. If the amount of matter is sufficiently great, this gravitational attraction could be strong enough eventually to halt the expansion altogether; the galaxies would then reverse their motion and come together, the universe ultimately undergoing a Big Squeeze. What would happen next is anybody's guess. One possibility is that there would be a Big Bounce and the universe would start to expand again. This is called an oscillating universe. If ours is a universe of this type, then perhaps what we call the Big Bang was not the moment of creation at all, but just the latest of many bounces. Indeed, perhaps the universe has always existed, perpetually bouncing for an infinite time in the past. According to one variant of this hypothesis, time is cyclic, exactly the same events being repeated in each expanding or contracting phase. According to another speculation, time might go backwards during the contracting phase. But regardless of the details as to what the behaviour of time would be during the two different phases, the important point is that we could conceivably be living in a universe that has no beginning and no end. If such were the case, all questions concerned with what happened before creation would be devoid of meaning – including the question of how God himself came to exist. Clearly, if it is legitimate to think of a universe that might have always existed, the same must be true of God.

Finally, let us turn to the question that triggered off the present discussion: the one about God being everywhere, paying attention to each of us, all at the same time. The first reason for regarding it with some suspicion is because of its use of the phrase 'at the same time'. At the same time according to whom? We have already seen that the concept of simultaneity has become somewhat shaky since the discovery that two persons who differ from each other in their relative motion, cannot agree on what happens at the same time. A second reason for believing the question not to pose insuperable problems has to do with an interesting suggestion, made some years ago, as to how one might account for one of nature's more puzzling features: the fact that every electron, neutron, or proton, is exactly identical to every other electron, neutron, or proton. The proposed explanation was simplicity itself: throughout the universe, there is only *one* particle of each type and it is the same particle that keeps popping up all over the place! This seemingly outrageous suggestion arose from further thoughts on possible similarities between space and time. The noted physicist and Nobel prize-winner, Richard Feynman, proposed that just as it is possible for a particle to be at one particular point in space at a number of different points in time, so it might be possible for a particle to be at one particular point in time at a number of different points in space. This ingenious idea for explaining the identical nature of the fundamental particles was taken very seriously for a while, though it does now seem to have fallen out of favour. My reason for telling you about it is simply to point out that whether or not there was any truth in the suggestion, it was an idea that could not be dismissed out of hand. There was no way it could be ruled out on the grounds of logic or commonsense. This being so, the proposal that God – like an electron, neutron, or proton – could be in a number of different locations at the same time is also one that needs to be taken seriously. This is especially the case when one finds Christians all over the world claiming to be in contact with the same God, all at the same time. The Christian view that individuals are of significance because their intrinsic worth is the subject of a continuing personal interest by a God who is to be found everywhere, is not one that can be reasoned away by logical argument. Like Einstein's theory, it is a view that stands or falls by the results of experimental test – in this case, the test of a life lived prayerfully.

In summary, therefore, our brief acquaintance with Einstein's theory of relativity serves to make a simple point: many seemingly intractable questions need not be the barriers to belief that some imagine them to be. To refrain from having a religious belief on the grounds that one needs first to have satisfactory answers to such questions, is a position that cannot be defended. As we have seen, the enlarged view of space and time afforded by relativity theory makes it highly unlikely that questions of this type have any meaning at all.

18 The Place of Paradox in Science and Belief

The point has now been reached where we must go to the very heart of Christian belief: its understanding of the nature of God and of Jesus. In our attempts to see how God relates to space and time we have already come across some of the difficulties. But there are others in store. The Christian idea of God is overlaid with paradox. ('Paradox' is a word that will figure prominently in our discussion; it signifies an *apparent contradiction*.) Knowing how to cope with paradox does not come easily to us. We all, to some extent, have been conditioned by our rational, scientific culture to think along straightforward logical lines. But strange to say, science, having taught us to think logically, now faces paradoxes of its own at the frontiers of the knowable. The fact that Christian belief has always been prepared to embrace an element of paradox, instead of trying to force the evidence to fit a neater, simpler conception, has now been revealed as one of its closest links with science and one of its greatest strengths.

In discussing the Christian understanding of God, I should perhaps point out that it is at the present time the subject of much lively controversy. It is not my intention, though, to become involved in this debate and I will instead confine my remarks to the traditional Christian viewpoint, giving some indication as to how the early church fathers came to formulate it.

The Christian idea of God had its roots, of course, in the God of the Old Testament – or at least God as he is portrayed in the later writings of the Old Testament. It is perhaps insufficiently appreciated that the Jewish conception of God was an evolving one. This conclusion is not immediately obvious because the writings of the Old Testament do not appear in chronological order. The first chapter of Genesis, for example, is a highly sophisticated, late piece of writing, dating from the time of the later chapters of Isaiah. Once the order is sorted out, however, the development becomes clear. At first God was thought of as a tribal god much like other tribal gods who were also thought to exist. He was concerned only for the welfare of his own people. He was a jealous and vengeful god. Later the Jews came to realize that there was not a multiplicity of gods at all – there was only one: a great and powerful creator God. Later still, on looking back over the way God had dealt with their nation, they came to see that he was righteous and just. Finally came the appreciation that he was also merciful – the petty tribal god having now been completely replaced by the great God of love.

That is one strand feeding into the Christian conception of God. A second came from the world of Greek thought. Though most Greeks believed there to be many gods, or none at all, an influential minority of intellectuals held there to be a single God. He was the unifying principle behind the world. To account for the way nature appeared understandable to the human mind, they claimed that underlying the order of things there must be a universal Mind. In contrast to the Hebrew god, who had developed into such an intimate and personal god as to be open to the criticism that he might have been unduly influenced by subconscious projections of childlike thoughts and feelings towards a human parent, the Greek conception of God was remote: though man could contemplate the Mind, it had no interest in him.

Christians owed much to these two sources, the one contributing an intensely personal creator God, the other an intellectually satisfying ground of all being. But this was just a beginning. To these was to be added the revelation of God through Jesus. Through their study of the scriptures, the early church fathers came increasingly to believe that Jesus was no ordinary man; in Jesus, God himself had become man. They could, for example, point to certain sayings of Jesus that appeared to indicate his unique position:

The Father and I are one.

. . . before Abraham ever was, I AM.

> Everything has been entrusted to me by my Father; and no one knows the Son except the Father, just as no one knows the Father except the Son and those to whom the Son chooses to reveal him.

> All authority in heaven and on earth has been given to me.

There are several other statements that point to the same conclusion. At Jesus' trial, the high priest demands of him, 'I put you on oath by the living God to tell us if you are the Christ, the Son of God'; Jesus replies that he is. When Jesus questions his disciples as to who they say he is, Peter replies 'You are the Christ, the Son of the living God'; Jesus accepts the title. There is the parable he told of the vineyard. According to this story, a man leases a vineyard to tenants. A succession of servants sent to collect the owner's share of the produce are beaten and killed by the tenants. The owner finally sends his beloved son, but he too is set upon and killed. The story concludes with the owner making an end of the tenants and giving the vineyard to others. The meaning of the parable is clear: the vineyard was a traditional symbol of Israel, the owner was God, the servants were the prophets, the beloved son was Jesus. This much was clear to the chief priests and scribes at whom the parable was aimed – and they reacted accordingly.

A further and subtle indication that Jesus saw his relationship to God as distinct from that of anyone else is to be found in the way he always spoke of 'My Father' and 'Your Father' – never of 'Our Father' (except, of course, when he instructed his disciples on how *they* should pray – a use of the word 'our' that did not include himself).

Then there was his claim to be able to forgive sins – a shocking assertion for anyone to make in those times; only God could forgive sins. He also assumed the right to amend the law of God: instead of 'an eye for an eye', he substituted 'turn the other cheek'; instead of 'love your neighbour and hate your enemy', he advocated 'love your enemies'.

But, without doubt, what convinced the early church more than anything else that Jesus really was the Son of God was the fact of his resurrection. This for them was absolute proof that he was no mere mortal – he was God in man and as such could not be held subject to death. The divine nature of Jesus was therefore seen by the early church fathers to be a feature they had to incorporate into their understanding of God.

The same was to happen in respect of their thinking about the Holy Spirit. Though they seem not to have devoted the same effort to discussing the nature and role of the Holy Spirit, it, too, was to become accepted as the embodiment of God himself. The Spirit of God had figured in the Old Testament and had been associated with manifestations of divine energy. But within the Christian church it assumed a special significance. At Pentecost, the disciples were seized by its power and its influence was universally felt throughout the early church as an upwelling of the power of God from within.

Thus the fathers concluded there to be a three-fold experience of God: he was to be worshipped as the heavenly Father (an amalgam of the Hebrew creator and Greek sustainer of the universe); one lived with him through the risen Jesus; one experienced him from within through the Holy Spirit. Or to put it another way: God over us, God with us, God in us.

The question then was how these diverse experiences were to be accommodated within a single, unique God. For although the fathers had come to accept that Jesus and the Holy Spirit were manifestations of God, they still clung strongly to the Jewish belief in monotheism.

Various solutions were offered. One held that the Father, Son and Holy Spirit were to be regarded as a more-or-less symmetric triad of persons, each having a separate function. This came perilously close to believing in three separate gods (a misconception about Christianity that is still common today). According to another view, God was one but had three distinct parts. This meant that none of the three parts was a full expression of God. Another suggestion was that God successively played three different roles, rather like an actor; another that there were three phases of his being (the Jesus phase now being finished, the Holy Spirit having taken over); yet another looked upon God as having a graded hierarchy with the Father as sovereign (the true God), the Son in a second and subordinate place, with the Holy Spirit occupying the lowest position.

None of these attempts to rationalize the conception of God was considered adequate. The fathers came at last to recognize that there really was no way out of the apparent contradictions. They simply had to be accepted as paradoxes. So, from their great Councils of Nicea (AD 325) and Constantinople (AD 381), they issued a creed, one that was to be affirmed throughout Christendom down to the present day:

> We believe in one God,
> the Father, the Almighty,
> maker of heaven and earth,
> of all that is seen and unseen.
>
> We believe in one Lord, Jesus Christ,
> the only Son of God,
> eternally begotten of the Father,
> God from God, Light from Light,
> true God from true God,
> begotten, not made,
> one in Being with the Father . . .
>
> We believe in the Holy Spirit, the Lord,
>   the giver of life,
> who proceeds from the Father
>   and the Son.
> With the Father and the Son he is
>   worshipped and glorified . . .

Out of this creed grew the doctrine of the Trinity. This doctrine held there to be one God and three persons: Father, Son and Holy Spirit. The persons are to be regarded as eternal and equal to each other. They are distinctive and yet in each the whole Godhead is operative.

I should perhaps mention in parenthesis that the word 'person', as used in this context, does not have exactly the modern meaning of the term. These days we regard a 'person' as a centre of self-awareness and, as such, he or she is separated from anything that is not part of that self-awareness. To apply that understanding of the term to the persons of the Trinity is once again to come close to the idea of three separate gods. Closer to the original intention of the word 'person' is our word 'mask'. But even here there is the danger of misunderstanding; by 'mask' we do not mean that God acts out three different roles behind three different masks, which he dons one after the other. Somehow, he plays all three roles at the same time.

Three in one, and one in three – a paradox indeed. It is a doctrine that does not really 'explain' God, at least not in the satisfying way we might have imagined a 'proper' explanation would do. It states who God is – namely, Father, Son and Holy Spirit – but does not show how we are to understand this union of contradictory qualities. In the circumstances, it is perhaps better not to regard the doctrine as an explanation at all, but rather as a framework within which thought, contemplation and discussion can take place.

Having agreed upon the doctrine of the Trinity, the fathers were next faced with the related problem of how one was to understand the nature of Jesus. As we have seen, they regarded him as the Son of God. But the same study of scripture as had led them to this conclusion, also pointed to his being man as well as God. For instance, he became hungry and thirsty; he grew tired and needed to sleep; he was tempted in the wilderness and on other occasions; in various situations he did not know what was to happen next (praying without knowing the outcome, being taken by surprise, expressing astonishment); he was so weakened by flogging that he was unable to carry his cross; at his crucifixion he plumbed the depths of despair crying out 'My God, my God, why have you deserted me?'; he died.

At first the fathers kept the two aspects of Jesus – the human and the divine – separate in their thinking. But then, under the influence of Greek intellectual thought, they felt the need to explain how the two aspects could reside within the same person. How was it, they asked, that Jesus could be both unchangeable, all-powerful, all-knowing and infinite God, and at the same time lowly man with his many limitations?

There were differing attempts at resolving the apparent conflict. One way out was to lay special stress on Jesus' humanity. According to this view, he was essentially no different from anyone else. All of us have the capacity to yield ourselves to God's will and allow him to take over the running of our lives. When we do so, we show others something of God's nature, his will and purpose. What was distinctive about Jesus was that he yielded himself so completely to God's will that we see in him the ultimate expression of God in human terms. The difference between him and ourselves is one of degree only. God in effect 'adopted' the man Jesus to be his son. Some saw this adoption happening from the moment of his conception, others dated it from the time of his baptism.

At the opposite extreme was the opinion that what needed to be stressed was not Jesus' manhood but his divinity: he was fully God; he only *appeared* to be a man. This view was particularly coloured by the Greek ways of thought. You will recall how the Aristotelian view of the world held there to be a world of imperfection and decay below the level of the moon and changeless perfection above. Accordingly, it was inconceivable that a divine being from the upper realm should become clothed in corruptible flesh belonging to the lower. Thus, Jesus' body could not have been normal flesh and bone – it only had the appearance of being a body.

Intermediate between these extremes were various compromise positions: Jesus was a created subordinate divine being; this made him both qualitatively higher than man and qualitatively lower than God the Father. According to another opinion, there existed within Jesus two persons: one human and one divine. Yet another held that Jesus' body and spirit were human but his mind was divine.

None of these interpretations gained general acceptance. Each was seen to be defective inasmuch as it ignored one or other vital aspect of the evidence. Gradually a consensus was reached that, whether it made intellectual sense or not, Jesus was to be regarded as both fully God and fully man. He was man in that he did actually suffer both physically and mentally and in this respect he was exactly as we are; he was God in that he was equal to God the Father and in this respect he was qualitatively different from us. Being equal to the Father meant that he, too, was eternal – he was not to be thought of as being created, nor coming into being at the moment of Jesus' conception. Though he was 'begotten' of the Father, this was not in the sense of having been begotten in time (so there would have been a time previous to that during which he did not exist), rather the word 'begotten' denotes the nature of the relationship between the Father and the Son. The moment of Jesus' conception was to be seen as that point in space and time at which the eternal, omnipresent Son of God identified himself with humanity.

These thoughts eventually found expression in the following form of words (issued at the Council of Chalcedon in AD 451):

> ... our Lord Jesus Christ is to us One and the same Son, the Self-same Perfect in Godhead, the Self-same Perfect in Manhood; truly God and truly Man; ... before the ages begotten of the Father ... acknowledged in Two Natures without confusion, without change, without division or separation – the differences of the Natures being in no way removed because of the Union, but rather the distinctive character of each Nature being preserved and (each) combining into One Person – not divided or separated into two Persons, but one and the same, Son and only-begotten God ...

As we found to be the case with the doctrine of the Trinity, so again we are faced with paradox. This Chalcedonian Definition, as it came to be called, like the former doctrine, did not really 'explain' anything. It did not say how the contradictory aspects of God and man were to be reconciled within the one person. Rather, it contented itself with spelling out the conditions that any legitimate discussion would have to satisfy if it were adequately to take account of all the evidence concerning both of the aspects.

These two declarations of belief – the one concerning the nature of God and the other the nature of Jesus – have been handed down to us as the definitive statements of Christian orthodoxy. This is not to say that they have gone unchallenged. As I hinted from the outset, there has been much debate about them in our own time. Certain biblical scholars, for instance, have called into question the scriptural basis upon which the early fathers built much of their discussion. Indeed, some scholars would go so far as to say that these statements have outlasted their usefulness; they were framed within a culturally conditioned way of thought that does not correspond to our own; they ought therefore to be replaced by a set of beliefs more in tune with current attitudes and knowledge. That is as it may be. I do not wish to be drawn. Instead I shall restrict myself to examining how the statements of Christian orthodoxy appear in the light of the paradoxes to be found in modern science. It is to the latter we now turn.

The most fundamental of the sciences is physics. Biology, chemistry, earth science, planetary science and medical science are all based on physics. And it is at the deepest levels of physics itself that scientists are now contending with paradoxes no less difficult than those encountered in the sphere of theology. It is no exaggeration to say that our whole understanding of modern science is ultimately rooted in these paradoxes.

Though reluctant to plunge you back into the deep waters of modern physics so soon after you have surfaced from those thoughts on relativity, I must. What you need now is a feel for some of the features of quantum theory. Once again I must ask the non-scientific reader to be patient and persistent. Quantum theory *is* a difficult subject – there is no doubt about that. But if you tackle the next half dozen pages with determination, perhaps re-reading passages where you fail to grasp their full meaning first time, I promise the rewards will be worthwhile.

Our starting point can conveniently be taken to be the question: 'What is light?' Light is, of course, the means by which we make most of our observations of the world, so it is important to understand what it is. At the beginning of this century, physicists thought they knew the answer: light was a wave. When a lamp was switched on, light travelled out from the bulb as a rippling sequence of waves – much like water waves caused by a stone dropped into a pond. This sequence of waves was made up of a succession of crests and troughs each smoothly joined to its neighbour, so creating an extended continuous phenomenon. The distance separating crests or troughs determined the colour of the light; blue light had a characteristic separation about half that of red.

All experiments into the nature of light could be explained in terms of this wave behaviour – all, that is, except one. The exception was an experiment concerned with the way light gave up its energy on being absorbed by matter. You may recall that earlier I mentioned how atoms consist of a central nucleus surrounded by electrons. When light falls on matter the energy originally contained in the light becomes absorbed by the electrons in the atoms. A close study of exactly how the electrons take up this energy reveals something very odd. Instead of all the electrons being gently nudged this way and that as the light wave passes over them – like a row of toy boats bobbing up and down on a water wave – most of the electrons are completely unaffected, whilst others absorb enormous amounts of energy, to the extent of being knocked completely out of their parent atoms. The electrons behave as though the row of toy boats had been subjected, not to an undulating wave which gently set them all in motion, but to a hail of gunfire which, whilst missing some boats, blasted others clean out of the water with direct hits. But how could this be? To accept that light was a stream of bullet-like particles would run counter to the wave interpretation attested by all the other experiments into light.

It was Einstein (again!) who championed the view that, regardless of this apparent inconsistency, the particle interpretation for light had to be taken just as seriously as the older wave interpretation. He showed that, according to the particle picture, the colour of the light determined not the distance between successive crests or troughs (which did not exist according to this picture), but instead, governed the energy of the individual particles. Blue light, for instance, consisted of particles possessing about twice the energy of particles of red light. Einstein's theory so accurately accounted for the details of the observed behaviour that there was no alternative but to accept that the particle picture was the correct way of explaining this last experiment. This result was considered to be of such importance that it was for his work into the behaviour of light that Einstein was later to be awarded the Nobel Prize, rather than for his work on relativity.

But this still left unresolved the problem of how the two conflicting pictures were to be married together to form an all-round understanding of the nature of light. Moreover, this uncomfortable 'wave-particle duality', as it came to be called, far from being something peculiar to light, began to spread! It spread to electrons. If physicists had earlier been confident that light was waves, they had been equally sure that they knew what electrons were: electrons were particles. The first reason for believing this is that they were constituents of matter. They could, for instance, be extracted from a metal ball by the powerful forces generated by an electrical spark. A metal ball being itself a particle, what more natural than to regard a piece knocked off it as also being a particle? Secondly, it was known that when electrons were in collision, they bounced off each other like tiny billiard balls. So it came as an immense shock to the physics community when, in the 1920s, new experiments revealed that beams of electrons possessed a wave nature. Despite the previously accumulated evidence that electrons were particles, under the conditions of these new experiments, electrons were found to behave like long, gently undulating streams of crests and troughs.

The same story was to be repeated for that other constituent of atoms: the nuclei. They too had originally been thought of as particles for the same reasons as electrons had been regarded as particles. But close examination of beams of moving nuclei revealed the presence of wave characteristics. For years, confusion reigned. All the basic constituents of nature seemingly led a Jekyl-and-Hyde existence, appearing sometimes as waves, sometimes as quanta (the general word 'quantum' being coined to describe the particle-like aspect of whatever type of radiation or matter was involved). The mood of the times was aptly summed up by one noted scientist in the comment:

> Physicists on Mondays, Wednesdays, and Fridays are using the classical theory, and on Tuesdays, Thursdays, and Saturdays the quantum theory.

Fortunately, the situation was not really as chaotic as *that* – not quite! In time it came to be recognized that the wave type of behaviour was consistently encountered in one particular class of experiment – that concerned with the way radiation (beams of light, or electrons, or nuclei) travelled from one place to another. Equally consistently, another class of experiment – that concerned with the way radiation interacted or collided with each other – showed behaviour that was always particle-like. Appreciation of this distinction went some way towards allowing one to anticipate the behaviour appropriate to different circumstances. But useful though this recipe-approach to physics might have been, it could hardly be regarded as a satisfying theory and did little towards answering the questions that had originally motivated these investigations: 'What is light?' and 'What are electrons?'

From this impasse there grew the suspicion that the paradoxical nature of the answers pointed to there being something fundamentally wrong with the formulation of the questions themselves. We have already seen how in the extension of physical theory to encompass high speeds, large masses and vast distances, questions once thought to admit of simple, direct answers, were found, in the light of relativity theory, to be nothing of the sort. Could it be that as we extend physical theory once more – this time into the atomic realm of the very small – that history is repeating itself and we have come across some basic flaw in the reasoning and assumptions lying behind our questions?

One man who thought so was the Danish physicist, Niels Bohr. Having already done much to advance the understanding of atomic structure, he directed his attention in the mid-1920s towards these investigations into the nature of light and of matter. In the process, he was destined not only to help solve these specific problems but also profoundly to alter our understanding of the goals of scientific enquiry in general. More importantly for us, though, he brought about a change in thought which, so I believe, has the deepest implications for the attitude we ourselves should be adopting towards our search for an understanding of God. This shift of thought can be illustrated in the following way.

Suppose we have an object that appears blue when we look at it in sunlight. We conclude: 'This object is blue.' In making this statement, we feel we have said something about the nature of the object itself. But if the same object is exposed to a yellow street-light at night, it looks black. (This is because a blue surface absorbs all colours except blue which is reflected; in the absence of any blue light – which is the case for the street-light but not for sunlight – the surface will absorb *all* the light and look black.) This being the case, should we not say: 'This object is black'? Alternatively, if we heat the object to a very high temperature, it will first glow red and then yellow (assuming, of course, it can stand the heat). So why should we not with equal validity claim: 'This object is red', or 'This object is yellow'? The reason is that everyone knows that when we state the colour of an object, it is understood that we are not being deliberately awkward and looking at it under a yellow light or heating it to high temperature. Nevertheless, if we are to be precise, our original statement, 'This object is blue', ought to be recognized as a much abbreviated version of: 'This object, when illuminated by white light, at normal room temperature, absorbs light of all colours except blue which is reflected.' In this pedantic, but precise form, we see that the statement is not actually saying anything about what the object *is*; it is saying how the object *behaves* under a given set of circumstances.

According to Bohr, this behavioural type of statement is the only type that can be made about nature; any assertion that, on the face of it, appears to be saying something about the intrinsic nature of an object, is in reality nothing more than a description of how the object is observed to behave when undergoing an interaction of some kind. It is therefore meaningless to ask the question 'What is light?' expecting an answer that tells us something about light itself – light in a state where it is not actively being observed through an interaction with its surroundings. All we can ever meaningfully ask is how light will behave in its interaction under specified circumstances. When questions are correctly framed in this manner, one discovers, as we have seen, that the answers fall into one or other of two broad classes according to the particular conditions specified in the question: either, 'Under the conditions of this experiment, light behaves in the manner known as wave-behaviour', or, 'Under the conditions of this experiment, light behaves in the manner known as particle-behaviour'. Thus the words 'wave' and 'particle' are not to be used as though they described what the object is; instead, they describe the nature of the *relationship* between the object and the experimental apparatus used to observe it. This, then, was the first important point Bohr was to make: we must switch the focus of our attention away from the object itself (whether it be light or electrons) and concentrate instead on questions about the nature of our interaction with the object.

The second point Bohr was to insist upon was that the two types of answer given to the questions (the wave-like and particle-like answers) were to be accorded equal status. Light must not be thought of as really a wave which sometimes only looked like a particle, any more than an electron was to be regarded as really a particle which sometimes only looked like a wave. He held that no further experimentation, however sophisticated, advanced, or ingenious, would in due course explain away one of these behavioural types leaving the other as the genuine solution. Both aspects must be fully embraced and treated on an equal footing. Together they afford complementary views; both are necessary for a full understanding. Indeed, 'complementarity' came to be the name given to this viewpoint.

Immediately, all the contradictions and inconsistencies thrown up by the wave-particle paradox disappeared. Nature's *behaviour* was perfectly consistent. In some kinds of experiment the characteristic behaviour was dependably wave-like, in others it was particle-like. One could never perform both types of experiment simultaneously on the same object because the two types of experimental conditions were incompatible with each other; thus one only ever got one or other answer – never both at the same time. The contradictions and difficulties only arose when one tried to go beyond the actual experimental observations and fuse the two types of result together in order to create a mental picture of what the object was. This extrapolation beyond the observations was what Bohr considered to be inadmissible. He claimed that the very nature of human knowledge was such that one had to stop short of such abstractions. Scientific man had to recognize that here was defined a boundary across which he would never pass. He would never pass it, not because he lacked the intelligence, or the mathematical skills, or because his computers were inadequate, or the necessary experiments were too complex or expensive to perform – he would never pass this boundary because there was simply nothing meaningful on the other side. This was no temporary frontier to current knowledge, destined one day to be pushed back further; *this was the frontier of the knowable.*

Bohr's views were revolutionary. They struck at the very heart of what was meant by scientific knowledge. He had called into question what had always been taken for granted as the final goal towards which scientific enquiry was striving. He was asserting that this goal was illusory and one had to learn to live with a type of understanding that fell short of the earlier supposed end-point. So deep were the implications of Bohr's thoughts that it took some time before the physics community discerned their true significance. When the realization did dawn, the storm broke. Scientists did not take easily to the idea that they and all their predecessors had been labouring under a misapprehension as to the very nature of the scientific enterprise. Einstein for one was not convinced. For twenty or more years Bohr and Einstein argued the issue in one of the most famous and keenly contested debates in the history of science. And the final result? Although Einstein himself was to remain unshaken in his belief that science would ultimately achieve its original goal of explaining, meaningfully, a world that exists independently of its relationship to us and how we interact with it, the victory, so it is generally agreed, went to Bohr. Though even to this day some people have their reservations, Bohr's interpretation of the nature of scientific understanding has come to be accepted as the correct one.

So what relevance does this latest excursion into modern physics have for our own discussion of the nature of God? We have already seen how the modern theory of relativity has cast doubt on many of the traditional questions asked about God – questions formulated on implicit assumptions about space and time which now appear unwarranted. Now we are led to enquire whether the new types of thinking that stem from modern quantum theory might also have a bearing on the assumptions which underlie questions aimed at trying to understand God.

Consider for a moment the question: 'Was Jesus really God or really man?' Is this the kind of question that seeks an answer in the form of a statement about the nature of Jesus himself, or is it content with an answer which merely describes how Jesus behaved in a given set of circumstances? Pretty obviously it expects the sort of answer: 'Jesus was really a man' or 'Jesus was really God' and as such requires a statement of who Jesus actually is, or was.

Whilst not wanting to jump straight to the conclusion that the only kinds of questions one can ask of God and of Jesus must be of a type similar to those that a scientist can ask about nature, it would be foolish not to recognize that scientists since Bohr have become wary of any seemingly fundamental question that expects an answer in the form: 'So-and-so *is* . . .' They have come to realize that, within the domain of science at least, such questions are meaningless and their lack of meaning is betrayed by the paradoxical nature of the answers given. Our question about Jesus is framed in exactly the form that quantum physicists in their domain would now reject as invalid. Moreover, attempts to answer it come up with conclusions that are in their way every bit as paradoxical as any faced by the physicists. Just as they had to contend with a form of duality involving incompatible alternatives, waves and particles, so we, too, in trying to understand the nature of Jesus, are faced with a duality involving equally incompatible alternatives, God and man.

The same kind of problem is encountered in the question: 'Who or what is God?' Again it is a question about being, rather than behaving. It therefore stands a good chance of being meaningless – an expectation apparently borne out by the paradoxical answers given in terms of the Trinity.

The more I think about such problems, the more I become convinced that most of the difficulties surrounding the Christian belief concerning God and Jesus arise from questions that have been incorrectly framed and, being so framed, generate false expectations as to what constitutes a satisfactory answer. We have yet to absorb the idea that at the truly fundamental levels of enquiry, any question that begins 'Who is . . .?' or 'What is . . .?' leads us up a blind alley. The way forward is through learning a lesson from the physicists. Like them we must distinguish those questions that are valid from those that are not. As we have had occasion to say before, we must not be misled into thinking that just because a question appears reasonable and makes grammatical sense it must necessarily be meaningful and open to an answer. Questions into the intrinsic nature of God and of Jesus are no more likely to be valid than the corresponding ones into the nature of light and of electrons. Just as scientists have had to come to terms with complementary behavioural descriptions of the fundamental physical entities, so we, too, have to content ourselves with complementary descriptions of God and of Jesus.

With regard to the nature of Jesus, for example, an examination of the gospels shows that in some circumstances he behaved as a man, in others as God; it was either one or the other, never both at the same time. As far as behaviour alone is concerned, there is no paradox – just as we found to be the case with electrons and light. The next step in understanding Jesus is to retain both types of behaviour in mind, emphasizing neither one to the detriment of the other – once again, just as was the case with electrons and light. Finally – and this is the most intuitively difficult step – we must come to accept that a full and proper understanding of Jesus consists of nothing more than holding these two complementary behaviours before us without in any way trying to force an unnatural and impossible fusion of the two.

The same remarks apply to our understanding of God. The knowledge we have of God does not relate directly to the nature of God himself existing, as it were, in isolation from us. What knowledge we have is that which comes from our interaction with him. As we have seen, Christians have a three-fold interaction with God: through the Father, the Son and the Holy Spirit. Whilst our attention is fixed on these separate modes of interaction there is no problem. The trouble comes when we try to go beyond the primary data relating to the interaction and attempt to deduce the nature of the God lying *behind* the interaction. It is this step which is invalid – or at least, I strongly suspect it to be so. After all, if physicists are not permitted to go beyond their interaction with electrons and say anything meaningful about an electron existing in isolation, can we really expect greater success when it comes to God? If such a move does not work for the humblest constituent in the universe, it is not likely to work for the creator of that universe.

Where do these thoughts leave traditional Christian teachings about Jesus and God? Surprisingly, they emerge unscathed. I say 'surprisingly' because, of course, there is in the Chalcedonian Definition of Jesus and in the Nicene creed no mention of the word 'behaviour'. And yet the spirit of these two statements is wholly in tune with what I have been saying are the lessons to be drawn from quantum physics. The crucial feature of the church's teaching about Jesus and God has always been its insistence on (i) the three complementary aspects (persons) of the one God and the two complementary aspects (man/ God) of Jesus; (ii) the need to accord each aspect equal status; and (iii) the need to refrain from contriving a false synthesis of these aspects in an attempt to achieve a simpler conception. Such attempts (for example, through regarding Jesus as really a man who only appeared sometimes to be God), were labelled heretical by the church fathers – just as, in our own century, alternatives to Bohr's views (for example, the electron was really a particle that only appeared sometimes to be a wave) also came to be rejected.

Acceptance of traditional Christian theology is no easy matter. The church's doctrines do not conform to our deep-rooted, preconceived notions as to what a decent, satisfying solution ought to be like. In this we are at one with physicists; they, too, find it difficult to reconcile themselves to the solutions offered by quantum physics. And yet the curious thing is that acceptance of this unfamiliar type of solution, paradoxes and all, can lead to new insights which are in themselves just as satisfying as anything one could otherwise have imagined. Let me try to explain.

The Christian God is pre-eminently a God of love. Love of its very nature must reach out to someone else. Once it turns in on itself and becomes self-love it degenerates into selfishness and self-indulgence, the attributes that are the opposite of love. For the greater part of time, the universe had no living creatures. During that stage of development, had God been a single entity, there would have been no love, for there would have been no one for God to love except himself. So, from the beginning, the existence of love required there to be a relationship of some kind. The overall unity of God had to embrace an inner self-relatedness. Creation, therefore, marked not so much the start of God's relationships, as the outward expression of the inner structure of his own being.

A second consequence of love being the overall characteristic of God is that there had to be a Jesus person. Love involves being able to identify with the other person; it involves sharing one's life, helping the other person, going through the same experiences together, tackling common problems and difficulties, having the same hopes and ideals; it involves sacrifice and pain. Without such deep involvement and commitment, the relationship can be at best superficial. If, as Christians believe, God is pre-eminently a God of love and, in particular, if he loves us his creatures, he cannot remain aloof and uninvolved. The proof of God's love for us is to be found in the life of Christ. It is not to be found in the gifts we receive from him, whether it be recovery from illness, or success in examinations or in one's work. Loving gifts these might be, but they do not, in themselves, prove God's love for us; if we have a mind to, we can always point to those aspects of our lives where things have not gone well and these can be reckoned as counter-evidence. No, the one conclusive proof is to be found in the life of Christ – in the way God involved himself in our lives at the grass-roots, in the way he suffered and sacrificed himself for us. That is the kind of expression of love that cannot be explained away. The over-riding requirement of love constrains the Godhead to have within it a direct and personal experience of the state of manhood. There *had* to be a Jesus person.

Another reason for finding the Christian understanding of God and Jesus gratifying lies precisely in the fact that they are complicated! Complication is something we should have expected. Throughout the realm of nature there exists a great variety of forms, extending all the way from a single electron, up through living creatures, to man himself. As one ascends the scale of complexity, there are smooth and gradual changes, refinements and touches of sophistication. But then, suddenly, one crosses a critical threshold at which the state of being undergoes a dramatic transformation and a previously undreamt of range of new possibilities opens up. For instance, an enormous gulf separates even the simplest single-celled organism from mere inanimate chemicals. Another large gap separates it, in its turn, from the multi-celled organism – the latter having the ability to develop specialized organs for performing particular functions and thus being capable of a much wider range of behaviour patterns. Still higher up the scale of organization, we come to man and once again qualitative changes occur, amongst them being the development of a spiritual capacity. So what do we expect when we consider God? Should we not anticipate the need to cross a further threshold? Surely we cannot expect him to be no more than a somewhat refined, improved and up-to-date version of ourselves. In some key respect he has to be *radically* different from us; in him we ought to see a new dimension to life opening up, a new and unanticipated potential revealed. In the doctrine of the Trinity we find the nature of that qualitative change: the *multi-person individual.* A remarkable conception indeed, one that is as far beyond the grasp of the human mind as the human being is himself beyond the imaginings of the lower animals. But any conception less radical would not have been worthy of God.

In these various ways, one can begin to perceive that acceptance of the complementary viewpoint, though giving rise to unusual and unfamiliar thought patterns, does not imply a rejection of reasoning.

Amid the paradoxes, one can yet glimpse a sense of order and inevitability about them.

Before closing, there is perhaps one further point I should add. You might well have thought I have been going a little too far in seeking to draw a comparison between the wave/particle paradox of physics and the kinds of paradox one comes across in theology. Have I not pushed the analogy beyond reasonable limits? In case this is how you feel, I end with this postscript.

In 1846, the Danish theologian Søren Kierkegaard asserted:

> When subjectivity, inwardness, is the truth, the truth becomes objectively a paradox; and the fact that the truth is objectively a paradox shows in its turn that subjectivity is the truth.

Kierkegaard was reacting against a wave of intellectualism that threatened to engulf Christian belief at that time. He claimed that one should not try to explain away the paradoxes – the ones we have been considering about the nature of God. Instead they should be embraced as pointing the way towards a new and more subjective kind of truth. He wrote:

> Let us take as an example the knowledge of God. Objectively, reflection (i.e. thought) is directed to the problem of whether this object is the true God; subjectively, reflection is directed to the question whether the individual is related to a something *in such a manner* that his relationship is in truth a God-relationship.

In advocating a move towards the more subjective form of truth so defined, Kierkegaard was paving the way for what I have been saying: the focus of attention should be shifted away from the contemplation of who God is, to how God relates to us, in other words how we interact with him.

Niels Bohr was known to have been an avid reader of Kierkegaard's writings. Though I cannot be sure he read the particular passages quoted above, I am struck by the resemblance between the views Bohr was later to advance in the field of physics and those put forward by his Danish compatriot some eighty years earlier. It is interesting to speculate that although I have presented the wave/particle paradox as an aspect of science that throws light on how we ought to be tackling the paradoxes encountered in Christian belief, historically it might well have been the other way round: twentieth century thought on physics might indirectly have been moulded by a nineteenth century theologian's contemplation of a fourth century creed.

19 Why Does God Permit Evil?

My attempt to offer some rational explanation as to why more than one person was required in the Godhead and why one of those persons needed to have direct experience of being a man, rested on the supposition that God's prevailing quality is love. The same conviction was earlier the basis for believing that Jesus had been compelled to perform miracles of healing. But this insistence on the perfection of God's love cannot be allowed to pass unchallenged. Even the most casual look at God's world shows that, in addition to love, there exists evil and suffering. Indeed, we have devoted much time to tracing its origins in the process of natural selection and in the indelible imprints left in us by past evolutionary struggles. How can God permit evil if he is as loving as Christians claim?

No one yet has come up with a wholly convincing solution; perhaps there is no answer that would satisfy everyone. I certainly do not put myself forward as an expert in the subject, being only too aware of the greater sufferings others have had to bear and how their experiences have led them to richer insights than I have. But there is one particular contribution to the discussion I can make through being able to draw on my background as a physicist. It is an indirect and unfamiliar approach to the problem but nonetheless, a helpful one – at least, I find it so. We begin, oddly enough, with the discovery of anti-matter.

Paul Dirac was an English physicist. By combining features from relativity theory and quantum theory he devised a fundamental equation for describing the behaviour of electrons. On solving the equation, he came across two distinct kinds of answer. One of these corresponded with the observed behaviour of electrons, the second appeared to be pure nonsense. This second type of solution intrigued Dirac; it seemed to imply that there ought to exist some electrons that behaved as though they had negative mass. This would mean that if you pushed on them they would come towards you, whereas if you pulled on them they would move away! No such behaviour, of course, has ever been seen. So what was one supposed to do with the offending solution?

Most people in Dirac's position would have ignored it as a silly mathematical quirk. But not Dirac. With a breathtaking leap of the imagination, he declared that the lack of evidence for negative mass electrons, far from proving they did not exist, showed that there were so many of them that they completely filled the whole of space! According to his proposal, negative mass electrons formed a uniform continuum permeating everywhere and everything; so-called 'empty' space was not empty at all – it was jam-packed with these strangely behaved particles.

To see how this seemingly preposterous suggestion could provide a solution to the problem of the non-appearance of negative mass electrons, we first look at a more familiar situation. As you sit reading this book, you are surrounded by air; there is air in your lungs, throat and nose, as well as outside you. If you are perfectly still and do not breathe (for a moment, at any rate) you are not aware of this medium. The only way to convince yourself that the air is there is to disturb it in some way. You might, for example, breathe heavily, the contraction of your lungs increasing the pressure and hence density of the air inside you compared to that outside. But now the air is no longer a uniform medium; there are more molecules of air inside your lungs than there are in an equal volume of air outside. A medium with a varying density cannot be a uniform continuum. As an alternative you might watch a feather drop; the fact that it falls very slowly is due to air resistance and that demonstrates the presence of the air. But air resistance is caused by the build up of pressure and density beneath the feather compared to that above and this once again has upset the uniform nature of the continuum. So we see that the only way to prove the air is there is to create irregularities in it; whilst the air remains completely uniform it cannot be detected.

Dirac's continuum was even more uniform than undisturbed air;

it was thought to suffuse not only space but also the interior of solid bodies – even the interior of atoms themselves. There would be no problem pushing one's way through it because the density of negative mass electrons would be the same in front as it was behind, or within; one would pass through the continuum completely unhindered. This is the property of *any* perfectly uniform continuum – it does not need to be one consisting of negative mass electrons. If one so wishes, one could imagine space filled with all manner of junk, provided there was enough of it and that it was present everywhere to exactly the same extent. I repeat: a perfect, uniform and undisturbed continuum is undetectable.

Were there no more to Dirac's idea than this, it would have attracted no attention. Scientists are not interested in theories that can neither be proved nor disproved. If there was no prospect of distinguishing between a space filled with negative mass electrons and one that was empty in the orthodox sense, there would be no scientific value to the suggestion. But Dirac did not leave it at that. He went on to point out that there was a chance of disturbing his proposed continuum and thereby showing that it did exist. Under certain circumstances, an exceedingly high energy quantum (or particle) of light might hit one of these negative mass electrons and knock it out of the continuum. The amount of energy gained from the light quantum would convert the negative mass into a positive one (a possibility allowed by relativity theory) and so would turn it into an electron no different from ordinary electrons. Being now a normal electron, it would become visible and behave in the conventional manner. But not only should we find this electron suddenly appearing as if out of nothing, it would leave behind in the continuum a 'hole' from where it had come. This hole would be characterized by an absence-of-negative-mass. An *absence* of *negative* mass? But that would be the equivalent of a positive mass. (If you have an account at a shop and it is in the red to the tune of ten pounds and if, for some reason, the shop-keeper cancels the debt, the absence of the debt is equivalent to your having received ten pounds.) So the hole would have a positive mass just like an ordinary electron and, as a result, become visible at the same instant as the electron that was knocked out of it. The hole would not itself be an electron; though its mass would be the same as a normal electron, certain other properties would have the opposite value. For example, an electron carries a quantity of negative electric charge. On jumping out of a continuum it would leave behind an absence-of-negative-charge and by the same kind of double negative reasoning we used before, we can see that this is the equivalent of a positive electric charge. So, whilst the electron knocked out of the continuum would have its normal negative charge (together with its newly acquired positive mass), the particle representing the hole would have the same positive mass as the electron but would carry positive electric charge.

No such positively charged electron was known at the time Dirac put forward his theory. Soon afterwards however, it was discovered and, furthermore, it was found to be created in exactly the way Dirac had predicted. It is now called the anti-electron. Dirac's leap of the imagination had paid off.

To summarize: a continuum that is perfect is undetectable; if it remains for ever perfect and undetectable it is a meaningless concept. The reality of the substance out of which a continuum is composed can only be manifested through a disturbance of some sort – a disturbance that necessarily destroys the uniformity, the perfection, of the continuum. Dirac's continuum was held to have no reality until it was possible to point to a hole in it – a place where the substance was absent.

At first it sounds odd having to point to something that is *not* what you are talking about in order to understand what it *is* that you are talking about. But it is not so. Certain philosophers who specialize in the study of human language and how it has developed hold that this is the very procedure by which we learn the meaning of words. Let me explain with an illustration.

I want you to imagine that we are invited into a house in a foreign country and we have no idea of the language. Our host decides to teach us the meaning of a few words. He begins by pointing to a cup and says a word – for the sake of argument, let us denote his word by 'A'. He repeats this word as he points to each cup. He reinforces the idea by shaking his head as he points to the saucers, tea-pot and plates to indicate that each of these is not an A. We now understand that A means 'cup'. He then points to a chair and says a second word – let's call it 'B'. The word is repeated as he points to each chair in the room. We are about to conclude that B means 'chair', when to our confusion, he goes on to point to the table and calls that a B too. He does the same with the settee, the coffee-table, the writing bureau, the bed and the stool. It begins to look as though everything is a B! But, no. After a while he shakes his head as he points to the car, lawn-mower, kettle, books, doors, windows, etc. In this way, we come to realize that B, instead of meaning 'chair', is the more general word 'furniture'. This discovery prompts us to reconsider whether we might earlier have been hasty in concluding that A meant 'cup'; might that not also have been a more general word: 'crockery'. No, we were correct; he had pointed to other items of crockery and shaken his head. Thus, we see that in coming to understand what both A and B meant, it was as important for us to identify objects not described by the word as those that were covered by it.

According to this theory of language and its meaning, what was true of the words 'cup' and 'furniture' in our illustration is equally true of many of the words we have learnt from our earliest days of childhood. It is true of the word 'love'. It is true of other words Christians use to describe their God – 'goodness', for example. To appreciate how meaningfulness becomes attached to words like 'love' and 'goodness' only through an acquaintance with their opposites, imagine if you will, a world entirely free of their opposites – a world in which suffering, evil, hatred and such like, are unknown. There is no pain or anguish, either mental or physical. Everyone has everything they could possibly desire, so there are no yearnings or deprivation. No one is less than wholly fulfilled. All behaviour is exemplary. Life is ideal. A perfect continuum of love and goodness. It is the kind of world that many believe a truly loving God would have created.

But had you been brought up in such a utopia, would you actually be able to grasp the meaning of the word 'love'? Under such conditions, how could those around you demonstrate their love for you? Bear in mind that you already lack nothing so they are not in a position to give you anything. You never suffer pain or illness so there is no occasion for them to care for you and show you sympathy. They cannot attend to your needs because you have none. They cannot tell you that they love you more than they love anyone else because that would entail other people feeling a sense of rejection through not being loved as much as you. They would not themselves be distressed at being parted from you, because their longing for you would be a form of suffering – which in this utopia is not permitted to them any more than it is to you. They cannot sacrifice themselves in any way for you because that too would cause them to suffer. They could, of course, show their pleasure at being with you, and possibly in making love to you. But as they are bound to do the same with everyone else they meet, what does such pleasure signify? Doubtless it could mean that they are having a good time, but that hardly helps you to understand what is meant by the word 'love'.

A paradise such as this, though at first appearance attractive, in reality amounts to empty nothingness. An eternally perfect uniform continuum of goodness and love must, by its very nature, be self-annihilating. Just as in physics the notion of an infinite continuum of negative mass particles acquires meaning only when it is possible to point to the particle's opposite number, the anti-particle, so an all-pervading goodness and love can only take on meaning when that perfection is broken and there is an encounter with their opposites: anti-goodness and anti-love. Logical necessity therefore, requires a measure of suffering and evil in the world in order that the positive qualities of love and goodness should be allowed to assume meaning.

Even an all-powerful, all-good, all-loving God cannot circumvent this kind of requirement. If, as Christians believe, the main purpose of our life on earth is that we should come to know and love God, then there must exist a potential for withholding that love. God, in creating love, must also concede to us a potential for rejecting him. Without that potential, his creation, which consists purely of love, has no meaning. And for that potential to be real, there must be those who deliberately choose to exercise that option and reject God and his ways – with all the consequences this brings for themselves and for others. It is not God who creates the evil; he merely opens up the possibility of our rejecting him; it is then our act of rejection that creates the evil; evil is *our* responsibility.

In this way, I believe, we can begin to discern why a loving God permits evil in the world he has created. It is not that he wants evil; it is simply that he has no alternative but to permit it if his own creation, love, is to acquire reality. This does not mean that God stands idly by and allows us to flounder in the misery of our own making. The troubles that man brings upon himself allow God to demonstrate his love for us. This he does in a variety of ways: he came amongst us in the form of Jesus to suffer alongside us and set before us an example to follow; he dwells within us in the form of the Holy Spirit giving each of us strength and guidance to resist evil and bear our troubles; and finally as our heavenly Father he assures those who genuinely turn to him of his loving forgiveness when they inevitably fall short of giving themselves wholly to him.

20 Destiny, Chance and Choice

Essential to the view that we can choose to love God or not as we wish, is the belief that we possess free-will. But are we, in fact, able to exercise choice? Someone who thought not was the French mathematician, Laplace. He once proudly boasted: 'Give me all the data on the particles and I shall predict the future of the Universe.'

Until the 1920s, this was a statement with which few physicists would have quarrelled. As far as physics was concerned, the world was little more than a giant machine governed by the laws of mechanics. Having been originally set in motion, it was inexorably and blindly working away in a completely predictable manner. The atomic particles that made up all the matter in the universe had each their particular position and motion at any given instant of time. Knowing these and the forces acting between them, one could, in principle, calculate the positions and motions of all the particles at any subsequent instant of time. Of course, in practice, one could never accumulate all the data necessary for making such a global prediction. But that was not the point. What mattered was that the state of the universe at any instant of time – and that included the human beings living in it – fixed all subsequent behaviour; the future was *determined*. This being so, it became hard to see how there could be any scope for free-will. With the future of the universe already fixed, there was no means of altering the course of events and so no possibility of exercising choice.

Then came quantum theory. For reasons I shall describe in a moment, the new theory was able to demonstrate that Laplace's strictly deterministic description of the universe was invalid; the prediction he had in mind was impossible to make even in principle. Not unnaturally this revelation was latched onto by certain Christian thinkers as the salvation of the idea of free-will. But were they right in so using the new physics?

To see what quantum theory had to say about determinism, consider the following. Suppose we wish to determine where a single sub-atomic particle, an electron, for example, will be found at some future point in time. To make this prediction, we need to know what its position and motion is now and what forces will act on it to alter its subsequent motion. (In a similar way, to determine when a train will arrive in a particular station, one needs to know not only where it is along the line now, but also how fast it is going and whether the driver intends to speed up or slow down.) To gain the necessary information on the electron, we must take a look at it and this, of course, involves shining a light on it.

Immediately we are in difficulties. We have learnt already that because of wave/particle duality, when light interacts with matter it behaves like a hail of gunfire. (Recall the analogy of the toy-boat being blasted out of the water.) Even if the electron is hit by only one bullet of light – and there must be at least one direct-hit for the electron to be 'seen' – then the motion of the electron will be disturbed; whatever it was before the collision, it will now be different. Fortunately there is a way round this problem: we make a suitable choice of illumination. You might remember that according to the particle description of light, the distinction between light of different colours lies in the energies of the 'bullets' – the redder the light, the less energy they carry. So, to measure the motion of the electron without disturbing it, we must use the reddest form of light available.

But this throws up a new challenge. According to the wave viewpoint, the distinction between light of different colours lies in the distance separating the crests and the troughs – the redder the light, the more they are separated and so, in a sense, the more the light is spread out. This characteristic of red light makes it difficult to know *where* exactly the light and the electron collide. As a result, red light, although suitable for finding the electron's motion, is a poor means of determining the electron's position.

We are now between the devil and the deep-blue sea. In order to predict the future behaviour of the electron, we need *both* the present position and the motion. But if we go for the reddest possible light and concentrate on determining the motion, we do it at the expense of making a good job of the position measurement. If, on the other hand, we go as far as possible in the opposite direction of the colour spectrum and use the bluest light to determine the position precisely, we knock the electron violently and lose all knowledge of its motion. We cannot have it both ways.

The idea of disturbing something by the very act of measuring it, is not of itself new. When the pressure in a car tyre is measured, a little of the air inevitably has to come from the tyre and into the gauge, with the result that the pressure being measured is somewhat reduced. A cold thermometer placed in a beaker of hot water will likewise extract some of the heat from the water and lower the temperature to be measured. These effects have no fundamental significance, however, because one can correct for them. If the volume of the space in the pressure gauge is known and compared to that of the tyre, a compensating allowance can be made. Similarly, by knowing how much heat it takes to raise the temperature of the thermometer, one can calculate how much heat has been extracted from the water and once again apply a suitable correction.

What was so startlingly new about the attempt to measure the position and motion of the electron was that there was no way to make the equivalent compensating correction for the disturbance caused by the action of the light. Repeatedly since the 1920s, physicists have sought a means of gaining precise and simultaneous knowledge of both position and motion and have failed. The impossibility of so doing has come to be recognized as something fundamental to the measurement process itself. It is given the name Heisenberg's Uncertainty Principle, after the German physicist who first formulated it. According to this principle, one can never hope to put together both pieces of information needed to make a precise prediction of the future behaviour of a sub-atomic particle; the most one can do is to specify the probability of various possible outcomes of future observations on the particle – the actual outcome being governed by chance.

Why the uncertainty principle should have been seized upon as the chink in the mechanist's armour is now obvious. For Laplace to be able to predict the future of the universe, he needed 'all the data on the particles', meaning their positions and motions. But the uncertainty principle denies that this is possible, even in principle. Thus it can be asserted that the world is *not* run on strictly deterministic lines.

But does this make the idea of free-will any more acceptable? I believe not; whatever the real answer to the free-will problem, this is not it – for two reasons. Firstly, in place of a strictly determined behaviour of sub-atomic particles, there is substituted, not choice, but chance. An electron faced with a number of possible locations at some future instant is eventually found to be in one of them. But how did it get there? Did it *decide* to go there? Of course not; it got there through random chance. So, if the idea is that our free-will comes through the operation of the uncertainty principle at the sub-atomic level – acting, for example on a particular atom located in a nerve-cell in the brain – then it is difficult to see what advantage has been gained in having particles behaving capriciously rather than deterministically.

In the second place, although it is true that determinism has disappeared at the sub-atomic level, it is still very much in evidence higher up the scale of complexity. The future behaviour of a sub-atomic particle might not be known, but the average behaviour of many such particles remains predictable. Take, for instance, the pressure in the car tyre we were considering earlier. The molecules of air in the tyre rush hither and thither, banging into each other and into the walls of the tyre. As each molecule hits the wall, it pushes against it and the impact helps to keep the tyre inflated. There are billions and billions of these molecules doing the same thing. Where and when each individual molecule will strike, or how hard the impact will be, we do not know. But providing there are a large number of these impacts taking place in each tiny interval of time, it is immaterial what the individual molecule does; we are concerned only with the steady average effect of the impacts – the steady effect known as 'pressure'. Now, it turns out that, even with the uncertainty principle operating at the sub-atomic level, a phenomenon like pressure *does* behave in a predictable manner. If, for example, the volume of air in the car-pump is halved by depressing the plunger half-way, then, assuming no change in temperature or loss of air through the valve, the pressure will now be twice its original value. This can be predicted and verified without problem.

Alternatively, we can take the example of the beaker of hot water. By saying the water is hot, we mean that its molecules are in vigorous motion, vibrating back and forth. The hotter the water, the more energetic these motions. Once again, we cannot keep track of the behaviour of the individual molecules. But what we can do is measure the average energy of all the molecules. This, in effect, is what we are doing when we record the temperature of the water; the temperature is a measure of the average energy of a vast number of molecules. And, like pressure, temperature is a predictable quantity. How it will vary with time as the beaker loses heat to its surroundings is something we can know in advance and later confirm.

The idea of something predictable emerging from occurrences that are themselves unpredictable is not, of course, new. When one tosses a coin, whether it comes down heads or tails is unpredictable. But if one tosses the coin many, many times, we can estimate that on half the occasions it will come down heads and the other half tails. Pressure and temperature are concepts similar to this estimate; they are derived from taking the average of many instances and so can be reliably predicted.

With regard to human choice, it is not at all clear which level of complexity and organization is involved in the initiation of the decisions we make. Are they triggered off by the action of an individual sub-atomic particle somewhere in the brain, or by the concerted action of a group of molecules? From our present rudimentary understanding of the workings of the mind, it is not possible to decide. Most people would probably consider it implausible that human decision stemmed from the action of a single atom. Atoms are, after all, unimaginably small – ten million of them are needed, for example, to stretch from one side of a pinhead to the other. For this reason, it might be thought that decisions are more likely to originate from a level of complexity where many atoms are involved – a level where the behaviour of matter can still be regarded as predictable.

If this is the case, then we see that, despite the lack of strict determinism at the sub-atomic level, it can yet be convincingly argued that our future behaviour is, by and large, fixed by what is going on now – much as Laplace originally claimed. So, from this, must we conclude that there is no such thing as free-will? Before making up our minds, let us turn once again to modern physics for further insight.

A lesson physicists have recently had to learn is the importance of not using concepts in the abstract, but relating them instead to specific viewpoints. In relativity theory for instance, we found that two events occurring simultaneously for one person were not simultaneous for someone else who was in motion relative to the first. It was not a question of one person being right and the other wrong – simply that the concept of simultaneity had no absolute meaning; it is a word that takes on meaning only when it can be applied to a particular viewpoint. Likewise, in quantum theory, an electron could be regarded as a wave according to the conditions of one kind of experiment and as a particle according to another. As with simultaneity and non-simultaneity, the concepts of wave and particle appear contradictory. What rescues the situation is that the contradictory descriptions derive from incompatible or complementary viewpoints. By this one means that no single observer can at one and the same time adopt both viewpoints: he cannot both be stationary relative to the events he is observing and also moving relative to them; he cannot be performing one type of experiment on an electron leading to the conclusion 'wave' whilst at the same time doing a quite different experiment which would yield the answer 'particle'.

These thoughts provoke the question as to whether the free-will/determinism problem might yield to the same approach. After all, in free-will and determinism we have concepts that are no less contradictory than those met in relativity and quantum theory. Could it be that there is no absolute answer to our problem, just as there is no winner in arguments about simultaneity or wave/particle duality? For this to be possible, we would have to regard the concepts of free-will and determinism as no longer describing something absolute, but rather as descriptions appropriate to two separate viewpoints. Moreover, these two viewpoints would need to be incompatible with each other so that one and the same person would never have occasion to use both words at the same time to describe his experiences. Two such viewpoints do exist and the concepts of free-will and determinism are in fact used in exactly this way. To see how this comes about, consider the following.

Imagine we have two people, one we call the investigator, the other the subject. The investigator sets out to determine the future behaviour of the subject. To this end he examines the contents of the subject's brain at the level appropriate to decision-making. He catalogues all the contents of the memory together with the natural in-born instincts to be found encoded in the subject's DNA molecules. (The experiment is, I hasten to say, hypothetical!) The study of the subject himself is then supplemented by an equally thorough investigation of all external influences – everything and everyone due to come into contact with him. The investigator is now furnished with all the information needed to allow him to give a complete description of the subject's future behaviour. The subject, to all intents and purposes, behaves like a programmed robot. It is to this cold-blooded dehumanized description – the kind that Laplace had in mind – that the concept of determinism applies.

But what of the subject's description of his own behaviour – how does it seem from his point of view? As each of us knows, an individual's experience of his own life is very different from what it might appear from outside. The subject needs to speak not only of his inter-relations with the outer world, but also of his perception of the private interior world he inhabits. He calls upon words such as: love, hate, envy, passion, fear, consciousness and so on – concepts that are at best inessential and possibly quite meaningless in the context of the external investigator's description. Among the new concepts is to be found free-will: the subject finds that an indispensible feature of his description is the idea that he has freedom to exercise choice. No matter how strongly the investigator insists that such freedom is illusory, the subject still remains convinced that the future is not fixed until he himself has decided what part he will play in shaping it. As Dr Samuel Johnson put it, in characteristically no-nonsense fashion: 'We know our will is free, and there's an end on't.'

But among the private interior concepts, that of free-will seems especially contentious. The external investigator need have no qualms over the subject's use of words like love and fear; if the subject chooses to label a complex set of inter-related atomic processes thus, then the investigator can have no objection. The fact that he, the investigator, has no need of such labels when describing the subject as a moving blob of chemicals implies no contradiction. But the subject's use of the word 'free-will' appears to challenge the investigator's use of the word 'determinism'. Here there does seem to be a contradiction. Is it not possible for the investigator to show the subject not only that his use of this concept is unnecessary (like the other interior concepts the subject uses), but in this case that the concept is actually *false*?

This is a crucial point in our argument. If we seek to solve the free-will/determinism problem by regarding these two words as applying to different viewpoints, then it is essential to demonstrate that the concepts cannot be freely transferred from one viewpoint to the other; the viewpoints must be incompatible, no one person being able to experience both simultaneously. We must be able to show that it is in fact impossible for the investigator to convince the subject that there is only one correct answer – just as it was impossible for the idea of simultaneity to be imposed on the viewpoint to which it did not apply.

To see whether the investigator can prove his point, we suppose him to carry out his investigation in the manner previously described. But now he records his predictions concerning the subject's future behaviour and seals them in an envelope. After the predicted events have duly occurred, the envelope is opened and the subject shown the record of the predictions. He discovers that, sure enough, his behaviour accorded exactly with what the investigator had beforehand calculated it would be. What would this prove? It would show that the investigator was extraordinarily clever, diligent and good at his job – but very little else. After all, one does not have to engage in a comprehensive investigation, such as the imaginary one we have described, in order to make a pretty shrewd guess as to how certain people will behave. A wife after twenty years of marriage can often predict unerringly how her husband will behave in any set of circumstances. The fact that she is invariably correct does not mean her husband is not exercising choice – merely that she is good at predicting what his choice will be. There is nothing in this to prevent the husband, in looking back on these moments of decision, believing that, had he had a mind to, he could just as easily have chosen to act out of character and done something different. And the same is true of the subject of our hypothetical investigation.

No, if the investigator is to prove to the subject that the latter has no choice – no genuine alternative to the action predicted – then he must provide the subject with the prediction *prior* to the event. If before the so-called 'moment of decision', the subject were told what his course of action was to be and he later discovered, when the moment arrived, that he was in fact powerless to act in any way other than that stated, then and only then, would the illusory nature of the 'decision' be proven; only under such circumstances would there be grounds for conceding a preference to the investigator's viewpoint and his use of the concept determinism.

But can such a situation be realized – can the subject be told *in advance* what his actions must be? The act of telling the subject must, of course, be counted as an external influence on him and, as such, it is potentially capable of affecting the final outcome. If the investigator is not careful, his act of communicating with the subject might invalidate his prediction. On the face of it, the way round this would be for the investigator to have already included in his prediction the effect of telling the prediction to the subject. This, however, will not do. An argument like this soon founders on logical inconsistencies. Imagine the subject to be an awkward cuss who resolves that whatever the investigator tells him, he will do the precise opposite! Our all-knowing investigator naturally would be aware of this intention, but what could he do about it? He might be tempted to provide the subject with the wrong prediction in order to provoke the desired final behaviour. But that defeats the aim of the exercise which was to inform the subject correctly of what his future actions would be. There is no way round the problem; the subject cannot himself be put in possession of an infallible prediction regarding his own future behaviour, even though that behaviour is known to the external investigator.

What this serves to show is that the investigator and the subject do indeed represent two mutually exclusive viewpoints. It is impossible for the investigator's view to be welded to that of the subject in order to produce a single agreed solution of the free-will/determinism question – just as it was impossible for the stationary and moving physicists, for example, to produce a single coherent description that would resolve the simultaneity/non-simultaneity question. In the same way as there is no final objective truth regarding simultaneity, so there is no objective truth regarding free-will and determinism. Both the viewpoint of the investigator and that of the subject are valid, each in its own way. Not a very satisfactory conclusion? Maybe not, but that is how it seems to be.

Finally, there is one more point to be made. Though once again we appear to have resolved an age-old problem with the help of insights drawn from the new complementary modes of thought developed for use in modern science, this is not really so. On examining traditional Christian thinking on the subject, we find the elements of the solution already there: free-will, determinism and their relationship to different viewpoints. The element of choice, as one might expect, is always much in evidence. Throughout the Bible, there is the constantly recurring theme that we must choose whether to follow Christ or not. The very meaningfulness of the concept of love, as we have seen, depends on there being a real alternative. The rationale of Christianity holds up only if we as individuals can exercise choice. So the situation as seen from our point of view incorporates free-will. But what of God's point of view? Does he await our decisions in ignorance of what they will be? Not so. The pattern of prophecies made in the Old Testament and fulfilled in the life of Christ presupposes events occurring in accordance with some pre-determined plan. This is made plain by St Paul when he says, 'For those whom he foreknew he also predestined'. The word 'foreknow' means 'chosen in advance' and 'predestined' means that God determined in advance the form our lives should take. Jesus himself, in describing the Last Judgment, speaks of the chosen as entering 'the kingdom prepared for you since the foundation of the world.' Thus, not only does the Bible affirm that, as far as we ourselves are concerned, we have freedom of choice, it also testifies that our choices are already known to God. In this way, we find the subject and investigator in our hypothetical experiment to be in much the same positions as ourselves and God respectively.

The doctrine of predestination has never been a popular one. Doubtless this was because of the difficulty of reconciling it with one's own direct experience of free-will. The fact that the church, nevertheless, clung to it despite what, I imagine, were many temptations to play it down was, I think, much to its credit. It is really only now – since we have begun to get used to complementary types of description in physics – that these old tenets of belief stand revealed as no longer contradictory, but rather modern in their outlook.

21 Only Wholeness . . .

In chapter 14, we saw that any object, from a Rembrandt portrait to a human being, could be described in various ways according to the context. In particular, we noted that when interested in questions to do with meaning and purpose we were invariably led to seek the answers at the highest levels of complexity and organization. At those levels, use is made of concepts like 'love', 'life' and 'spirit' – concepts that do not seem to figure at the lower levels where it is more appropriate to talk in terms of the energies and positions of sub-atomic particles and the forces between them. It is now time to look at these higher concepts in more detail with a view to trying to understand their nature. We do this using fresh insights which have emerged from quantum theory.

But before doing that, let us first attempt a more conventional approach. We begin by trying to explain a relatively simple example of a higher concept: pressure. This is a term that is unlikely to appear in the vocabulary of, say, an atomic physicist, but is one we all use when, for example, pumping up tyres. Does this mean that the term 'pressure' introduces some novel feature that the atomic physicist might be expected to know nothing about? Pressure, as we saw earlier, comes about as the result of tiny impacts between individual gas atoms and the walls of the tyre. The number of these impacts in any interval of time is so great that the average force exerted on the walls remains essentially constant. For this reason, it becomes convenient to coin a new word. And why not? If all one is interested in, when pumping up the tyre, is the averaged-out effect rather than the details of each and every atomic impact, then it is only sensible to deal in terms of pressure. But this new word does not imply that something new has been added to our understanding. The atomic physicist, in his detailed study of how each atom behaves, is perfectly capable of adding up all the individual contributions and arriving at the same averaged-out effect, if he so wishes. Indeed, far from adding anything new, the concept of pressure has thrown away a great deal of the information that was available at the atomic level. The word 'pressure' is the lazy man's way of dealing with what is, in truth, a very complicated situation. Its justification lies in its convenience, rather than in any ability to contribute new understanding.

The same is true of the concept of temperature. Each atom or molecule possesses energy as it rushes about or vibrates. The temperature of an object, as we have already pointed out, is just the average of all these individual atomic energies – the greater these energies, the higher the temperature. Once again, it is a term that introduces nothing new – rather, it is one that dispenses with unnecessary details and provides a succinct summary of whatever it is we actually need to know.

How about the concept of colour – the colour of some object? You remember in our discussion of the Rembrandt portrait, at the level of individual electrons and nuclei there is no meaning to the idea of colour. When one reaches the level of atoms and molecules, however, the forces between sub-atomic particles come into play and one can speak of the distances separating the particles. On taking these into account, it begins to make sense for us to talk of the object as being able to absorb light of some colours and not others (through re-arrangements of the particles relative to each other). In this way the object takes on a characteristic colour of its own. 'Colour', therefore, although a higher concept that is not just an averaged-out effect of what the sub-atomic particles are doing individually, can nevertheless be understood in terms of sub-atomic particles, their interrelated positions and the forces between them.

The success we have had in explaining 'pressure', 'temperature' and 'colour' in terms of the behaviour of the sub-atomic particles encourages us to apply the same approach to all other higher concepts. Take for instance 'life'. Because life is such a very high concept, we would doubtless be well advised to tackle its understanding in stages. First, as we have done before, we would define life to be the group of characteristics known as respiration, nutrition, reproduction, growth, excretion and responsiveness. Then we would take a look at each of these characteristics in turn and examine the nature of the chemical and physical processes that underlie them. Finally, we could seek to describe these processes in terms of the behaviour of the sub-atomic particles. We might tackle a concept like 'love' in the same way, identifying the physiological changes that usually accompany the phenomenon (heart pounding, pupils of the eye dilating, for example) and accounting for these in terms of electrical signals passing along the nervous system and chemicals being released in certain locations.

There are those who maintain that this is all there is to these concepts. 'Pressure' and 'temperature', 'love' and 'life' – they are merely useful terms for gathering together, in some convenient form, those general features of the basic atomic processes relevant to some particular purpose. No new element is introduced by these concepts, all the information being already contained in the detailed lower level descriptions of the individual sub-atomic particles and the way they are assembled together. Such a view sees the progress of science as one in which these higher concepts are progressively explained away in terms of ever more basic descriptions at lower and lower levels. (It is the familiar reductionist line of argument again.) Furthermore, it is an argument that would claim that any higher concept not open to an explanation in terms of a set of atomic processes – a concept like 'spirit', for example – must be one devoid of meaning.

How sound is this reasoning? Is it really the case that all aspects of the behaviour of large groups of atoms, such as a human being, cannot be anything more than the sum total behaviour of its constituent particles? The answer is no. To see why, we have to look once again to the kind of thinking that has grown out of quantum theory.

You will recall that Bohr and Einstein, those two great physicists who had each contributed so much towards building up the new physics, were ultimately to find themselves in profound disagreement over the true meaning of what had been achieved. Bohr, you will remember, believed that physics had to confine itself to making statements about our interaction with the world; Einstein wanted to restore the idea that the goal of physics was to describe the world itself, independently of our interaction with it. Bohr was later to develop his ideas further and it is this extension to his thoughts that we are now to examine.

We begin with Heisenberg's uncertainty principle – the principle that denies the possibility, even in theory, of being able to gain completely precise information on the position and motion of some object such as an electron. Previously we explained the uncertainty principle in terms of what might be called the 'clumsiness' of the measurement process. We tacitly assumed that out there somewhere was an electron which at any point in time had a well-defined position and motion. The problem arose when we tried to take a look at it to find out what that position and motion was. The act of taking a look involved firing a quantum of light at it. The nature of the interaction between the light and the electron depended upon the particular kind of light used.

If we were particularly concerned to get a good fix on the position of the electron, we needed to have light tightly bunched together, with the distance between the wave crests and troughs very small; this pointed to the use of blue light. But blue light, we noted, was associated with highly energetic quanta, so this meant that each time contact was made with the electron, it was knocked flying, so ruining any determination we might have made of its motion. Alternatively, the use of red light, with its less energetic quanta, made it possible to measure the motion, but because of the way its crests and troughs were spread out, not its position.

At no time did we doubt that the electron actually did *have* a position and motion. It was just, if you like, our bad luck that whenever we tried to extract the information, we inevitably ended up with less than the full amount. In this way, we had to make a distinction between how the electron actually behaved (existing at a precise position and possessing a precise motion) and the maximum information our measurements could yield about the electron's behaviour (information subject to the limitations imposed by the uncertainty principle).

This was how most physicists, Heisenberg himself included, were initially inclined to interpret the significance of the uncertainty principle. But in the late 1920s Bohr came to the conclusion that there was a deeper meaning. His new thoughts on the subject grew out of earlier discussions of the wave/particle paradox. The resolution of that paradox had come about by shifting the focus of attention away from the electron itself and fixing it instead on the interaction between the electron and the experimental apparatus used to observe it. The electron was no longer regarded as being either a wave or a particle; the words 'wave' and 'particle' described the nature of two different types of interaction one could have with the electron.

Pursuing this line, Bohr now declared that all the terms used in physics are similarly derived from observations. What applies to the words 'wave' and 'particle', applies equally to the words 'position' and 'motion'. Just as we cannot speak of the electron as actually existing in the form of either a wave or a particle, neither are we justified in regarding the electron as actually existing at some particular precise position with some particular precise motion. The words 'position' and 'motion' only take on meaning in the context of making a specific observation; they arise out of the descriptions we give to identifiable interactions with the electron. Transferring the words 'position' and 'motion' from the description of the interaction to a supposed description of the electron itself was to be regarded as a misuse of language. Any statement purporting to speak of the actual position and motion of the electron must, by its very nature, be devoid of sense.

Heisenberg was among those who were quickly won over to Bohr's new way of thinking. Not so Einstein. He was convinced Bohr was wrong and he determined to find some loop-hole in his reasoning. Initially, the form of his attack lay in trying to devise ways round the uncertainty principle. If he could produce just one experiment capable of providing more precise estimates of the position and motion of the electron than those permitted by the principle, he would have gone a long way towards demonstrating that the electron really did possess a precise position and motion. The uncertainty principle would then be shown to be what was originally thought to be the case, namely, that it was just a guide as to how close our observations could generally get to determining what those values of position and motion were.

Repeatedly Einstein thought he had succeeded. He would describe some ingenious experimental arrangement which, at first sight, appeared capable of yielding the desired precise information. But each time, Bohr, with the help of his now close colleague Heisenberg, was able to uncover some flaw in Einstein's arguments. Again and again, the uncertainty principle stood vindicated and with each new demonstration of its validity, more and more physicists were won over to Bohr's viewpoint. Increasingly, it came to be accepted that the reason why one could not measure simultaneously both a precise position and a precise motion for the electron was that such things did not in reality exist.

Then came a dramatic switch in tactics. Having finally run out of ideas for circumventing the uncertainty principle, Einstein launched an attack from a different quarter. It was a remarkably clever approach – one destined to spur Bohr to the ultimate achievement of his scientific thought. Though it made no claim to get round the uncertainty principle, Einstein's new argument did appear to demonstrate that there was invested in the electron more information than was being extracted by the observations. Though it is not easy to reproduce Einstein's reasoning in a digestible form, here is a simplified version, based on an analogy, which might be helpful.

Imagine a school-teacher responsible for keeping order in the playground. Suddenly there is a commotion over in one corner and he hurries there to investigate. On arrival he finds a boy flat on his back, clearly knocked over by someone else. What can the teacher conclude about the person responsible for the accident from looking solely at the condition of the boy on the ground? Obviously it must have been quite an impact to have felled him. The culprit must have been either very heavy, or running fast, or both. But there are no heavy people about, only children, so it follows the culprit must have been running. Not only that, he must still be close to the scene of the accident because there has not been time for him to get far from where the other boy is lying. That at least narrows the field down a little. Thus, even before questioning any one in an attempt to identify the person responsible, the teacher has learnt something about him; he has an idea of the speed with which he was running and roughly where he is to be found now – all from an examination of the victim.

This simple incident contains the essence of Einstein's approach. What he did was to set up an imaginary situation in which two particles, for example, two electrons, were to be in collision. As a result of the impact, the motion of each electron is modified. If, for instance, one was stationary to begin with, then its motion afterwards would clearly depend on how fast the other one was going. So from studying the change in motion of one electron (let us denote it by the letter V, standing for 'victim', in analogy to the boy who was knocked over), the experimenter can deduce something about the speed with which the other electron, C, (standing for 'culprit') has rebounded. If he wishes, he could measure V's motion precisely and this would yield a precise determination of C's motion. Note that he is able to do this without actually looking at C directly. On the other hand, the experimenter, by looking at the position of V, rather than its motion, could deduce something about the position of C – and again, this determination can be made as precise as one wishes and without having to look directly at C. In either case, whether one uses the measurement on V to yield an indirect estimate of C's precise motion, or alternatively of C's precise position, one can later go ahead and perform a direct measurement on C to confirm that the indirect estimate was correct. Einstein's master stroke was this: on leaving the collision, electron C does not know which experiment is subsequently to be performed on V, whether it will be the one giving a precise estimate of position or the one giving a precise estimate of motion. Electron C must, therefore, take away from the collision precise information on both the position and the motion in readiness for whatever type of measurement the experimenter later decides to perform. In this, Einstein envisaged that once the impact between the particles was finished and they were moving apart, there could be no further interaction between them and therefore no new information could be exchanged. It would be impossible for electron V, in effect, to say to electron C, 'Hey, he has just done a precise measurement of my motion so he knows what your precise motion ought to be; here is the result he got, so be prepared in case he wants to check it out with you directly.' By then it is too late. Electron C can only be in possession of whatever information it originally took away from the collision and, as Einstein cunningly argued, that must be no less than precise information on both aspects.

Einstein was not claiming to have got round the uncertainty principle; he had not shown how both pieces of information could be simultaneously obtained – the experimenter had still to choose whether to go for precise position or precise motion – but what he had done, apparently, was to demonstrate that electron C had actually to possess both pieces of information. In this, Einstein was making a statement about electron C itself, as opposed to a statement about an interaction with electron C, and this was the kind of statement that Bohr had held to be impossible to formulate meaningfully.

Within six weeks of the appearance of Einstein's argument, Bohr had published his refutation! He countered that Einstein's whole approach to the problem was invalid. It was inadmissible to regard the two electrons as separate autonomous entities – two distinct physical systems, only one of which (electron V) was being observed, the other (electron C) being left unaffected. By one and the same measurement, the experimenter was extracting information about both particles. The system he was interacting with was not a system consisting solely of the single electron V, but a different one that embraced both particles. Even if the two electrons were too distant from each other for there to be any force or influence operating between them, they could not be regarded as independent of each other. Here, Bohr was going even further than he had done before. Previously he had confined his thoughts to situations in which only one basic particle, an electron, was under examination. And, as we have seen, in that situation he showed that all that could be meaningfully said concerned an interaction with that electron. Now he was saying that if instead of one electron there were two and if it appeared that information was being extracted about both, then the only meaningful statements that could be formulated were those about an interaction with a two-electron system – not a one-electron system with a second one-electron system being left unaffected. And this was the case whether or not the two electrons were in contact with each other in the conventional physical sense.

This conclusion is nothing short of amazing. Of all the remarkable thoughts we have met in this book – those arising from evolution, cosmology, relativity – I believe nothing compares with this. It runs counter to almost all previous scientific thought. Throughout the ages, science has relentlessly pursued the reductionist line, seeking always to analyse and break down phenomena into their component parts – my own line of research being the spearhead of that movement today. Once nature has been dissected to reveal its elemental components, one has only to add the knowledge of how they are assembled piece by piece and held together by physical forces, to achieve full understanding – or so it seemed. Now Bohr was challenging this view. He claimed that putting the components together (in the case of Einstein's proposed experiment, the two electrons), one produced a combined system that had characteristics that could not be explained as merely the sum of the separate components and the physical forces between them. In interacting with this combined system, one encounters a quality that stems purely from what can only be described as its 'wholeness'.

Einstein could never bring himself to accept this. Until his death in 1955, he continued to hold out against Bohr's ideas. Even today, fifty years on, experiments are still being performed and new ones devised to test the truth of Bohr's claims (the weight of experimental evidence, incidentally, being strongly, if not completely conclusively, in favour of Bohr). From time to time, the old arguments are taken out and given another airing. But, by and large, modern physicists have come to accept that ultimately the reductionist line fails and the element of wholeness needs to be restored.

What relevance does all this have for our earlier attempt to assess the significance of the higher concepts? Why did I claim that quantum theory opens up the possibility of there being higher concepts that cannot be explained away in terms of the physical properties of sub-atomic particles? Quite simply this: physicists have found that in trying to deal with what is, after all, the simplest conceivable composite system – one involving just two electrons so far apart from each other that no force, electrical or gravitational, operates between them – it is incorrect to regard it as consisting of just one electron and its properties added to the other electron and its properties; one must, in addition, take account of the connectedness of the system – a quality that has no explanation in terms of the tangible physical forces that are normally regarded as responsible for connecting otherwise separate entities. This being so, ought we not also to be taking into account this quality of wholeness when studying the composite system that is of interest to us – the human being? Can we seriously believe that if physicists cannot give a satisfactory description of two non-interacting electrons in terms of the old reductionist way of thinking, we are likely to fare better when dealing with the billions upon billions of atoms, closely bound together by physical forces into intricate structures, that go to make up the human being?

The fact that one cannot legitimately account for a composite system in terms of progressively adding together the contributions of component parts casts doubt upon the validity of our earlier attempt to understand the higher concepts. Concepts like pressure, temperature and the colour of an object, might well continue to yield to this kind of description, but whether we are justified in extending the same approach to all the higher concepts is another matter. Particularly this is so of those concepts that apply exclusively to the whole person and cannot be thought of as applying in part. For example, though one may speak of the pressure on one's right big toe being greater than that on one's left – because of a shoe that is pinching – it clearly makes no sense to think of one's right big toe being more in love than one's left. Though one's ears might be colder than the rest of one's body, one cannot think of them as being less keen on some course of action than some other part of one's body. The qualities of love and of choice are attributes that are applicable only to the whole person. This is a new factor that must be borne in mind – a distinction that sets these additional concepts apart from the earlier ones. Bohr's revelation that the attributes of a system considered in its entirety are not those of its component parts, opens up the possibility that these additional concepts – the ones exclusively associated with the whole person – can assume an authenticity born of that wholeness and integration.

Another point. One of the reductionist arguments was that any concept that did not have a readily identifiable counterpart in the physical, material world – the concept of 'spirit' for example – must be devoid of meaning. But how convincing is this now to be regarded? After all, that which binds a composite system together in the sense envisaged by Bohr has nothing to do with normal physical forces. Indeed, it is extremely difficult to conceive the nature of this non-physical connectedness – a difficulty that has militated against the easy acceptance of Bohr's views. But our successful description of the way we relate to the world nevertheless demands that we do use the idea of connectedness. That being the case, it seems to me hard to sustain the position that the concept of spirit ought to be discarded merely because it too appears to have no directly corresponding physical manifestation.

None of this *proves* that we have a spirit, or that concepts, such as love and free-will, are necessarily something more than a way of referring to the averaged-out effects of lots of atomic processes – like pressure and temperature. All I am saying is that Bohr's discoveries in the field of quantum theory have profoundly changed the climate of thought in physics. It is a change that I believe is directly relevant to our own considerations, in that it makes more acceptable the idea that the concepts that have figured in our own thoughts might be endowed with an import far deeper than anything we would otherwise have dared to ascribe to them.

Perhaps the most fitting end to a discussion like this is provided by some words of Friedrich von Schiller, the German dramatist and poet. Though spoken in the eighteenth century, so clearly having nothing to do with quantum theory, they have an uncannily modern ring about them:

> Only wholeness leads to clarity
> And truth lies in the abyss.

Not surprisingly, it was a favourite saying of Bohr.

22 In Conclusion

The time has now come to gather the threads of our discussion and try to form an assessment of the present-day relationship between science and belief.

In the first place, we discovered that there was nothing in the so-called 'confrontations' of the past to indicate any fundamental rift. These conflicts were not what most people now believe them to have been, namely, examples of old religious claims being subjected to scientific scrutiny and being found wanting. The trial of Galileo was about the pride of a Pope, thoughtlessly wounded by an over-zealous scientist lacking in tact; it was not about any great theological issue. The reception accorded the theory of evolution by natural selection arose because Christians were reading the Bible in ways its authors had not originally intended; it was not that the claims of the Bible had been exposed as fraudulent.

Important though it was to clear away such misconceptions, this was but a prelude. Later we were to discover that what emerges the more strongly from any comparison of the scientific and religious endeavours is not so much the differences that divide them, as their similarities. Repeatedly, we found that theological studies of God, the creator, were being answered with resonant chords from the scientific study of his creation. This showed up particularly when ancient truths were found to have anticipated some of the findings of modern science.

Recall, for instance, the doctrine of original sin. Whilst every natural instinct protested the innocence and essential goodness of the new-born child, the Christian message unswervingly held that each of us has a tendency to pursue our own selfish ways, contrary to God's wishes – a tendency that is there from our earliest days. Only now, with the help of the molecular biologist and the psychologist, do we begin to recognize how this comes about: the way the law of the jungle – that self-centred instinct towards putting one's own survival first – is written into our DNA molecules from conception; the way we are unwittingly led by our parents and close relations to regard ourselves as the centre of attraction during those vital, impressionable first years of life.

There were the questions to do with space and time. The writers of the Bible described God as transcending space and time and Jesus as both living in time but also in some sense beyond it. Pure nonsense in terms of the narrow scientific notions of their day, but in keeping with what can be now glimpsed through the mind of Einstein.

Long before physicists, Christian thinkers had contended with the need to incorporate an element of paradox into understanding sought close to the frontiers of the knowable. Whether one is dealing with the time honoured paradoxes (freewill/predestination or the God/man duality of Jesus), or the modern ones found in physics (simultaneity/non-simultaneity or the wave/particle duality of the constituents of nature), the resolution of the paradoxes comes in the same way: both elements of the paradox must be accorded equal prominence, neither one being emphasized at the expense of the other, and each is to be seen as related to a particular view-point.

Finally, whilst scientists pursued the reductionist line, seeking to explain everything away in terms of the behaviour of ever smaller constituent parts, Christians maintained that there existed higher concepts that could not be adequately described, or indeed accounted for at all, at these sub-atomic levels. Today, through the work of Bohr, scientists have also come to an awareness of the need to restore the quality of 'wholeness'.

Thus, repeatedly, we have found the latest scientific discoveries and modes of thought foreshadowed in the ancient truths. But this has not always been the case; the flow of ideas is two-way. Much of the new science serves as an inspiration to deeper reflection on the part of the theologian. For instance, I believe further thought should be given to the spiritual nature of man as it must now be viewed in the light of the theory of evolution. Did the spirit suddenly come into being at some arbitrary stage of the evolutionary process, or did it gradually evolve from an earlier primitive form? If so, what exactly could be the nature of this primitive form? Should one not argue that animals today might possess rudimentary spirits and so be capable of experiencing an after-life of sorts? An animal's ability to question why it is here, to ponder over the existence of God and to develop a relationship with God – all surely essential to a spiritual life – might be insubstantial, but a possibility that perhaps ought not to be ruled out altogether. The difference between man and the animals might be one of degree rather than of kind.

Modern science exposes facile and false 'proofs' of God's existence. Many Christians, however, still point to the presence of life as a proof of God's existence, seemingly unaware that this is but a variant of the now discredited 'God of the Gaps' approach. Ought they not to learn the lesson of the past and think again about this – before being forced so to do by scientific discoveries yet to come?

The scientific outlook, whilst not ruling out the possibility of miracles, does make it more difficult for modern man to accept them uncritically. So many people are put off Christianity by the mistaken impression that all the miracles must be accepted lock, stock and barrel. I would like the church to make it plain which miracles are considered to be essential.

Lastly, there are questions provoked by our new understanding of the nature of knowledge. We have seen how modern physics steers us away from trying to make statements about an objective world existing in isolation from us – instead, we are required to fix our attention exclusively on our interaction with the world. Though I have argued that a doctrine such as that of the Trinity already implicitly contains this philosophy in its formulation, people do, nevertheless, continue to try and make statements about God as he *is*, rather than restricting themselves to descriptions of how we interact with him and he with us. I suppose one of the reasons for this is that Christians believe that God has an objective existence and this is in no way dependent upon our interaction with him; he does not suddenly come into existence the moment we choose to think about him. Christians are suspicious of subjective views of God which permit everyone, in effect, to believe whatever they like about him – one person's views being accounted as good as another's. But restricting one's thinking to our interactions with God need not entail any denial of his objective existence. A physicist does not have to believe that the world goes out of existence the moment he shuts his eyes and stops observing it. All that modern physics requires is the recognition that whatever form of existence the world has when not being observed, we are powerless to formulate any meaningful statement about it. And the fact that meaningful statements in physics are confined to our interactions with the world, does not imply any subjectivity of the kind that would grant each physicist the right to get whatever result he likes, all results being counted equally valid. There still remain true observations of the world and false ones. Thus, I believe, theologians today ought to be prepared more explicitly to recognize that all valid statements they make about God are statements about our relationship with him and that any attempt to go beyond that, in order to arrive at an objective description of God himself, is inadmissible. There can be true statements about our interaction with God and false ones. The objectivity of Christianity is preserved not in submitting to the test supposed assertions about God himself, but in determining the truth of the statements we are allowed to make about our interaction with God.

So we see, in a variety of ways, science and religion working together, each shedding light on the other, sometimes one showing the way forward, sometimes the other. This comes about not only because the modes of thought they use are similar, but also because they are both based on the same methodology – one rooted in experiment. We have seen that confirmation of the central belief of Christianity, the resurrection, comes not from persuasive argument, nor from blind credulousness, but from an act of faith incorporated into an experiment – the experiment known as prayer. Faith used in this way is no different from that employed by scientists in their own investigations and the confirmation provided to those engaged in the experiment is no less certain.

But this is not to say that there is no difference at all between scientific and religious enquiry; that would be going too far and, in any case, there is no reason why they should be identical in all respects. Their chief difference is to be found in the fact that, whereas someone like myself can be totally convinced of the reality of God, there can be someone else, equally sincere, who is not. Such a conflict of opinions, though common on questions to do with religion, is seldom encountered in scientific discussions (though even in science, differences do sometimes arise, as witness the confrontation between Bohr and Einstein). As a scientist, I expect, in general, to have no difficulty in convincing others of the reality of physical concepts – concepts like mass, electric charge and charm. I do this by pointing to the experimental evidence that was earlier responsible for convincing me. But as a Christian, I find the final clinching proof of God's existence is not of this external kind that can be jointly examined and appraised; it is part of my interior world of certainties – it is to be found alongside the other internal perceptions: love, fear, hope, pain . . . All these perceptions are to me just as real and true and irrefutable as the perceptions I have of external experiences – those experiences I can share with others. But though these internal experiences are real to me, no one else can gain access to them, others having to rely on equivalent perceptions of their own private interior worlds.

This inability on my part to argue others into believing in God, in the same way as I can argue a colleague into accepting that charm exists, is something I find hard to accept. It is so frustrating! But deep down I know it has to be this way. The establishment of a relationship with God is all to do with love and no one can be argued into loving another. Unlike the discovery of a new property of matter, each of us has to perform the God-relationship experiment for ourselves – it cannot be left to the experts, it cannot be done by proxy. The most I, or anyone else, can argue, is that each person owes it to him or herself to give it a try.

The sad fact is that most people never get around to it – at least, they do not tackle it with the determination that stands a chance of securing a successful outcome. In this respect, I feel science has much to answer for. In a quite unexpected way, it has unintentionally worked against religion. Science spawns technology and technology surrounds us with many marvels and gadgets, transforming our life-styles, making them more complex and sophisticated – and, in a sense, artificial. We forget that we are animals, no different in terms of evolutionary development to our cave ancestors. Whereas they had no option but to face each day the harsh realities of life – the need for shelter, food and clothing and the ever present threat of death – we, in contrast, all too easily find ourselves distracted from those things which really matter. Our attitude towards death, for example, so often assumes an air of unreality. Cocooned by wonder-drugs, kidney machines, heart transplants and a host of other aids for combatting disease and infirmity and for prolonging life, we lull ourselves into thinking that death has been banished – rather than merely postponed. The products of science and technology conspire to put from us the sense of urgency that ought to consume us over all questions of an ultimate nature – those related to religion and to the purpose of life. I say 'ought' because, if Christianity is right, it throws a new perspective on life – one that reveals the kind of life we should be living, rather than the one we probably are. It is not that people are actively against religion; opinion surveys are forever reporting that most people have a belief in a God of some sort, albeit a belief that generally has little or no discernible effect on their lives. As I say, it is not that people are against religion, it is simply that they never actually get around to giving the matter the serious consideration it deserves. There are so many other things in their lives that demand attention and that appear more pressing; the question of religion seems to be one that can be safely left to a later time when there is more opportunity for mature reflection. Except that it is then left too late.

An advantage of being a scientist is that this inclination to sit on the fence is not one to which we are particularly prone – we come off it one side or the other. I suppose it is because when one spends all one's working life asking deep, searching questions about the nature of the world, it is difficult not to go that one step further and ask why it is all here and what, if anything, lies beyond. Among the ranks of scientists are to be found atheists and Christians, but very few waverers in the middle. Over the years, there appears to have been a tendency for the atheists to be the more outspoken and, as a result, they have succeeded in creating in the public mind the impression that scientists as a body share their views. But this is not so. In a seven-man research team to which I recently belonged, for example, there were three of us who were committed Christians. One was very active in church affairs, another was later to give up a highly paid job as a senior physicist in an international laboratory to become a priest on one-sixth of his former salary, and I, whilst continuing as a scientist, became a church lay reader. Nor is this exceptional; only recently another friend of mine, this time a distinguished professor of physics at Cambridge, relinquished his post in order to go into the ministry. It is actions such as these that speak more eloquently than all the words and arguments I, or anyone else for that matter, can muster. It is in the lives of professional scientists who are also Christians that one finds the most convincing answer to the question of whether science and belief are compatible.

List of References

List of References

Page v 'two rivers . . .' from 'Selected Portions of the (Rhapsodic) Sea' by L. Houston, published in *A Stained Glass Raree Show*, Allison and Busby 1967. Used by permission of the author.

5 Adam and Eve story, Gen. 2.4–3.24. (All biblical quotations are taken from *The Jerusalem Bible*, unless otherwise stated.)

5 For a modern account of the theory of evolution by natural selection, see e.g. *Evolution* (a selection of articles from *Scientific American*), W. H. Freeman 1978.

7 'To suppose that . . .' see Charles Darwin, *On the Origin of Species*, Everyman Library 1956, p. 455.

8 To learn more of cosmology, you might like to look at J. Silk, *The Big Bang*, W. H. Freeman 1980.

10 'I see no good reasons . . .' Charles Darwin, op. cit., p. 167.

11 Augustine's views on this subject are to be found in *De Genesi ad Litteram* and in *De Trinitate*. For a discussion see, for example, E. Gilson, *The Christian Philosophy of St Augustine*, Gollancz 1961, pp. 197–209.

20 'God fashioned man . . .' Gen. 2.7.

45 A comprehensive account of miracles is given in *Miracles in Dispute*, E. and M. Keller, SCM Press 1969.

47 Temptations in the wilderness, Matt. 4.1–11.

47 'It is an evil . . .' Matt. 16.4.

47 Reference to Jonah, Matt. 16.4; Matt. 12.39–42.

47 Rich man and Lazarus, Luke 16.19–31.

48 Moses feeding the Israelites, Ex. 16.1–36.

48 Casting out devils, see e.g. Matt. 9.32–34; Mark 9.14–29.

48 Walking on water, Matt. 14.22–32.

48 Jesus feeding the multitude, Matt. 14.15–21; Matt. 15.32–38.

49 Turning water into wine, John 2.1–12.

50 Jesus on the seashore, John 21.1–7.

51 'Yahweh your God . . .' Deut. 18.15.

51 The suffering servant, Isa. 52.13–53.12.

51 Crossing the Red Sea, Ex. 14.15–31.

116 'The sun rises . . .' Eccles. 1.5.
116 'High above, he pitched . . .' Ps. 19.4.
127 'The heavens declare . . .' Ps. 9.1.
133 There are several good popular books on relativity. See e.g. M. Gardner, *Relativity for the Million*, Macmillan.
147 'The Father and I are one' John 10.30.
148 'Before Abraham ever was . . .' John 8.58.
148 'Everything has been . . .' Matt. 11.27.
148 'All authority . . .' Matt. 28.18.
148 'I put you on oath . . .' Matt. 26.63.
148 'You are the Christ . . .' Matt. 16.16.
148 Parable of the vineyard, Mark 12.1–12.
148 Claim to forgive sins, see e.g. Luke 5.20–21; Luke 7.48.
148 'Turn the other cheek' Matt. 5.38–42.
148 'Love your enemies' Matt. 5.43–44.
149 Pentecost, Acts 2.1–13.
151 Jesus hungry, Matt. 21.18; Mark 14.12–16;
          tired, Matt. 8.23–25; Luke 22.44;
          praying without knowing, Luke 22.41–42;
          expressing astonishment, Matt. 8.10;
          unable to carry cross, Luke 23.26.
151 'My God, my God . . .' Mark 15.34.
154 There does not seem to be any popular book on quantum theory that goes into the subject sufficiently deeply to search out the philosophical implications that we need to draw upon. The most appropriate treatment is *Science and Belief: From Darwin to Einstein, Course A381*, Block IV, Units 7 and 8, Open University.
156 'Physicists on Mondays . . .' a quotation by Sir William Bragg.
165 'When subjectivity . . .' S. Kierkegaard, *Concluding Unscientific Postscript*, Princeton University Press 1941.
174 A good discussion of the problem of free-will, and many other topics concerned with the relationship between science and religious belief, is to be found in D. M. MacKay, *The Clockwork Image*, IVP 1974.
180 'We know our . . .' Boswell's *Journal* for 17 October 1769.
183 'For those whom he . . .' Rom. 8.29 (Revised Standard Version).
183 'The kingdom prepared . . .' Matt. 25.34.

Index

Index